IMAGES
OF THE
KENNET & AVON

100 Years in Camera

Bristol to Bradford-on-Avon

Niall Allsop

REDCLIFFE
Bristol

For Kay . . . and a river shared

First published in 1987 by
Redcliffe Press Ltd, 49 Park Street, Bristol 1

ISBN 0 948265 91 4

Typeset by Dorchester Typesetting Group (Bristol) Ltd
and printed by Redwood Burn Ltd, Trowbridge

CONTENTS

Front Cover: A horse-drawn narrow boat on the canal at Bath.

INTRODUCTION

One hundred yards downstream of Hanham Lock an imaginary line separates the waters of the Bristol City Docks from those of the British Waterways Board's River Avon Navigation. Such a line of demarcation is as meaningful as the various appellations that have been attached to the waters on either side since the beginning of navigation between Bristol and Bath in 1727.

The waters of the river Avon have coursed this valley since time immemorial and respect no such partitions. The Kennet & Avon Canal was not cut to link Bath and Newbury because these were seen as two great commercial centres but rather as a means to link the existing Kennet and Avon Navigations which in turn established trading routes to Bristol, London and beyond.

Thus this collection of photographs starts in Bristol's bustling 19th century dockland in the knowledge that, though not strictly part of the Kennet & Avon, it is as much a part of the story of the boats and people that worked and played on the Kennet & Avon as each lockful of water that joins the river Avon at Bath.

THE KENNET & AVON: Images in Camera

On December 15th, 1977, a lone motor cruiser arrived at Bath's Pulteney Weir from Swineford. Amid the clicking of cameras a plaque was unveiled at its landing place to commemorate the first barge-load of goods to work through the newly completed Avon Navigation 250 years earlier. The enthusiasm and good intentions of those who chose to remember the occasion fell generally on deaf ears, ears untuned to the significance of the cargo of 'Deal-Boards, Pig-Lead and Meal' that marked the beginning of a new era back in 1727. And why should it have been otherwise? Communication in the 1970s was all about speed and technology – carrying by water was hardly going to excite wide interest, particularly as the popular image of the river was either as a rich man's playground or a flooding nuisance.

But back in the early 18th century the natural wildness of the river incited like passions in man and, in a time of uneven and uncertain road transport, offered an alternative trade route between Bristol and Bath which in turn could open up greater and more varied markets. Later the same century, as the transport revolution progressed, man-made water routes were being cut the length and breadth of the country, heralding a Canal Age that was to spawn a broad swathe across the south of England to link Bristol with the Thames: the Kennet & Avon Canal.

Talk of making the Avon navigable between Bath and Bristol goes back as far as the Elizabethan era . . . to a time when few would have recalled that the river, like others before the ascendency of the miller, had enjoyed the passage of 'Ships or Boats of Good Burthen' up to the post-Conquest period. The manipulation of the river for power rather than passage had, however, become the rightful order of things and, aided and abetted by the vociferous fears of established farmers and traders and the gentry – the latter unimpressed with and even fearful of the prospect that the navigation would 'bring down the dearness of provisions complained of by all persons who frequent the Bath' – all attempts to upset the status quo failed.

The dawn of a new century brought with it an entrepreneurial zeal which, coupled with the technology of the pound lock that could facilitate a compromise between power and passage, was to fulfil a dream long held by the influential citizens of Bath. Nevertheless the Bill that eventually received the Royal Assent on May 22nd, 1712 for the purpose of the 'clearing, making and effecting a Passage for Boats, Lighters, and other Vessels upon the River Avon' itself suffered from opposition despite the fact that it was promoted by Bath's corporation. Not everyone was seduced by the aspirations of the Bill and its claims that it would be 'very Beneficial to Trade, Commodious and Convenient for the Persons of Quality and Strangers (whose resort thither is the principal Support of the said City of Bath) advantageous to the Poor, and convenient for the carriage of Free-stone, Wood, Timber, and other Goods and merchandizes, to and from the said Cities and Parts adjacent . . .' with the result that the corporation did not feel able to embark upon the project until the mid 1720s.

By the time work on the navigation formally got under way in April 1724, three names were at the forefront of the scheme: John Hobbs, a deal merchant from Bristol; Ralph Allen, Bath's postmaster and an enterprising quarry owner; and John Hore of Newbury, employed by these two and their thirty fellow 'Proprietors of the Navigation between Bath and Hanham Mills' in the 'direction and chief management of the works'. Coincidentally, Hore had cut his engineering teeth on the Kennet Navigation, completed in 1723; as he supervised the work

1747: John Padmore was the architect of the Great Crane erected in Bristol docks in 1735; Padmore also engineered the tramroad from Ralph Allen's quarries at Bath. *Port of Bristol Authority.*

on the Avon did he ever, even momentarily, cast his mind's eye eastwards to the homely Kennet and wonder whether one day these two might be united? A romantic notion, perhaps, but no less far-fetched than the 1626 logic of Henry Briggs who advocated a Thames-Avon link based on his discovery that at one point the 'rivers' are a mere three miles apart!

As it is likely to have been Hobbs' deal that made up that first cargo to Bath, it can be assumed that at least two of his fellow proprietors traded in pig-lead and meal; likewise Ralph Allen was quick off the mark with his trade in Bath stone from his quarries above Bath at Bathampton Down and Combe Down. But all of this was pre-empted by the enterprising Samuel Tonkins who, in 1727, even before Twerton Lock (now more commonly known as Weston) was completed, was operating a 'new Passage Boat between Bristol and Twerton'. Some 13 years later this self-styled 'first and only waterman of Bath and Bristol river' announced that he had added three new boats to his fleet, 'with a house on each, with sash windows' and that two boats did the journey daily in 'about' four hours at a fare of one shilling. Perhaps it was one of the Tonkins' craft that was the gaily decorated wherry that brought George II's daughter, the Princess Amelia, from Bath to Temple Back in May 1728. The Princess, known for her dislike of bad roads and having already suffered the journey from London to Bath by sedan chair, seized on the opportunity to give the Royal seal of approval to the newly opened navigation. Fed and watered by the dignitaries of Bristol, Amelia and her entourage were hauled back to Bath . . . not by horses but by gangs of men paid to pick and pull their way along the towpath-less river bank.

It would be a mistake to see the traffic solely in terms of carrying between Bristol and Bath, though it goes without saying that much of the trade on the river would have been localised. John Hobbs, for example, may have been 'the chief instrument of making the river Avon navigable' to Bath but he was no less active as a merchant trading with foreign parts than was Ralph Allen an exporter of freestone to Belfast and Dublin. Thus was Bristol's busy dockland the focus for transhipment in both directions, though some traders cut out the middle man and worked what were essentially coastal craft up-river to Bath. One such traffic was in Shropshire coal which passed down the Severn in trows and in so doing displeased the Somerset colliers who saw their own livelihoods threatened. Suspicion alone links their plight with the threats made to the navigation in the early 1830s and, despite the introduction of the ultimate deterrent for wilful damage to the works of a navigable river and warnings published by the Navigation's proprietors, sabotage occurred. In his *An Essay towards a Description of Bath,* John Wood described the event thus:

> 'But notwithstanding this, between the Hours of Eight o'Clock, on Thursday Night, and Four o'Clock on Friday morning, the 15th. and 16th. of November, 1738, the Lock at Solford [sic] was almost destroyed by Persons unknown; who left two threatning [sic] Papers, which declared in Substance, That an Attempt was made only by Three Hundred Men, as the beginning of much greater Mischief that was intended against the Navigation, by as many Thousand, unless an immediate Stop was put to the sending of any more Coals by Water.'

Such was the strength of feeling and unity amongst the 'Persons unknown' that not one of the three hundred nor of the thousand in the wings was ever brought to justice; their point made, no further such disturbance occurred.

1820: The first Prince Street Bridge, built in 1809 to replace one of the dock's several ferries, was one of the improvements associated with Jessop's 'Float'. *Canal Tavern Collection.*

While the Avon Navigation flourished, Bristol was going through a self-inflicted crisis and as the 18th century progressed the inadequacies of its tidal facilities became the more apparent; too late Bristol Corporation sought to improve these, to seize back the initiative usurped, as they saw it, by others. Ideas were also being mooted at the eastern end of the navigation that eventually led to the Western Canal project which foresaw the extension of the river navigation Thames-ward. Thus, as the century was drawing to a close, the extremities of the navigable Avon were poised to witness enormous changes.

Back in the 13th century Bristol had pulled off a coup with its diversion of the river Frome, an enterprising stroke of genius that soon established it as a major port, the more so when its western-facing location proved to be such an important factor in the discovery and exploitation of the New World. These works remained the basis of Bristol's wharves, quays and docks for 500 years before the influential Society of Merchant Venturers acknowledged that 'the keeping of the Vessels always afloat in the Quay and Back of Bristol would be a scheme productive of the most beneficial consequences to the city'. Various schemes were

1835: William Muller's view of the 'Float'. Although the original course of the Avon has been tamed, it retains a river-like quality. *Bristol City Art Gallery.*

1827: T L S Rowbotham captures the drama of the fire at the Tucker Street sugar refinery by Bristol Bridge. Round the corner from the Porter Brewery (later George's) were many of the wharves that traded up-river with Bath. *Bristol City Art Gallery.*

debated and argued over during the second half of the 18th century, a time-consuming exercise that in no way helped stem the tide of frustration for those who could lose more than half a year's potential trade through having to work around the vagaries of the ebb and flow. It was thus not until 1803 that the scheme 'for Improving and rendering more Commodious the Port and Harbour of Bristol', presented by William Jessop the previous year, became law; it was a further six years before the merchants of Bristol were able to take full advantage of their new Floating Harbour. The tide had turned . . . or had it?

Though notions of eastern extension of the navigable Avon were broadcast during the late 18th century, the prospect of navigation up-river to Chippenham did not generate great enthusiasm. In Kennet country it was a different story. Here the river had been navigable between Reading and Newbury since 1723 and as the benefits it brought to its adjacent communities became the more obvious so, too, did the logic of extension westwards. Though initially this was mooted in terms of navigation only as far as Hungerford, by July 1788 the 'logic', as advertised locally, soon embraced 'an Extension of the Navigation of the Rivers Kennett [sic] and Avon, so as to form a direct Inland Communication between *London* and *Bristol,* and the West of *England,* by a Canal from *Newbury* to *Bath*'. With a strict directional bias the project was known as the Western Canal; it was not until 1793, when the proposed route was re-surveyed by John Rennie for a second time and his more southerly route via Great Bedwyn, Devizes and Trowbridge approved, that the name was altered to the Kennet & Avon Canal. The following year 'An Act for making a Navigable Canal from the River Kennet, at or near the Town of Newbury, in the County of Berks, to the River Avon, at or near the City of Bath; and also certain Navigable Cuts therein described' duly received the Royal Assent.

Thus, as another new century crept into the history books, was the stage set for increased exploitation of the trading potential of the river Avon from its new non-tidal base at Bristol to its man-made extension from Bath to Newbury, Reading and beyond.

By its very nature the river was unpredictable and prone to flash flooding; nor were the scenic qualities of its circuitous route any compensation for trade lost to an innate wildness . . . hitherto accepted as a necessary evil. Canals were a cut above all this so it can hardly have come as a surprise to the Avon's proprietors who, having played hard-to-get in 1795 when the Kennet & Avon Canal Committee tried to purchase the river navigation, now found themselves facing a proposal to build a rival Bath & Bristol Canal. The proposal actually got onto the Statute Book in 1811 but, faced with an unhealthy economic situation and considerable local opposition such as that expressed at a protest meeting held at the Crown Inn Saltford that 'the line of the intended Canal runs in the most destructive direction for the landowners', the project was shelved. Involvement in the Bath & Bristol Canal had not impeded the K&ACC in its clandestine acquisition of Avon Navigation shares to a majority shareholding and its commitment, in 1812, to the long-overdue construction of a horse towing path alongside the river.

The Kennet & Avon Canal was opened as far as the Devizes locks on November 10th, 1810. The *Bath Journal* reported the occasion thus:

> 'Friday – a barge loaded with 40 tons of stone passed the locks for the first time from the river Avon to the Kennet and Avon Canal, near this city; and we understand that 30 days working weather will so far complete the canal, that boats of 40 or 50 tons burthen may pass from Bristol to London without shifting. The guns on Sydney Wharf were fired on the above occasion.'

In his *Annals of Bath (1830–34),* Roland Mainwaring records that barges containing more than 800 sacks of flour also arrived at Sydney Wharf from Newbury (the unfinished locks at Devizes presumably having been by-passed via the adjacent tramroad) and that 'On this freightage six horses were employed; while, on a moderate computation, the draught by land carriage would have required more than one hundred!' Such basic statistics were as much of a phenomenon of this new enterprise as the fact that the weather held and the canal was opened throughout on December 28th, . . . not quite the 'before Christmas' that one advertiser in the *Bath Chronicle* predicted in furtherance of the sale of four barges and four narrow boats, the latter having previously carried coal between Birmingham and Newbury.

With the final link in the waterways chain between Bristol and London thus forged and other connecting narrow canals such as the Somersetshire Coal and the Wilts & Berks also open, a barge or narrow boat was all that was needed to become, in contemporary parlance, a 'Bath and Bristol carrier'. Since the opening of the Avon Navigation such carriers had traded largely between Bristol's Temple Back and the Quay (the prefix 'Broad' was not used before 1819) at Bath. Long before the notion of eastward extension was mooted, river carriers such as John Price, Simmonds & Partners, John Veal, Walter Wiltshire, John Parsons, Thomas Bascum, Samuel Ward, William Collins and Cornelius Cutler traded beyond the limits of the navigation. It would seem, however, that few of those who were still trading towards the end of the 18th century had either the capacity or inclination to exploit the virgin canal link to Bradford-on-Avon and beyond, a link that brought so many new carriers – perhaps even a new breed of carrier – onto the river at Bristol and Bath.

1829: Bath's Quay and Old Bridge, the centre of the city's waterfront trade. *Victoria Art Gallery, Bath.*

The exception was Samuel Ward who traded from the Quay at Bath for about a quarter of a century from 1790. In 1805 he was one of four 'proprietors' who had warehouses on the Quay which saw 'barges continually passing and repassing to and from Bristol on the River Avon, which convey goods at about 7s per ton.' All four were essentially merchants trading in one particular commodity – Messrs Bond and Penny were corn factors, Williams was a brewer while Ward was a salt merchant – and their barges would have been largely geared to serving *their* needs above all else. Supervising the quayside activity was John Salmon, an employee of the 'River Avon Company' until the early 1840s and for a time a carrier in his own right. In addition, with the opening of the canal, John became the Bath agent for Bristol-based carriers Thomas Parsons & Co while brother Jacob was likewise looking after the Bath interests of Richard Horner, who, alone among the four river-based carriers at Bath, had not previously been involved in bankruptcy proceedings. The remaining two, Euclid Shaw and Baker, Jorden & Co, also had Bristol bases and, like the others, took full advantage of the concept (if not the reality) of the Bristol-to-London link; 'superior water conveyance' in 'Kennet & Avon Barges' with 'Regularity and Dispatch' and 'without Shifting' would have been a familiar composite advertisement for their services. Much too would have been made of the fact that, compared with the equivalent road carriage, it was more reliable and certainly cheaper; in May 1810, with the opening of the route between Bath and Devizes (save for the Widcombe locks, alongside which there was a tramroad), Richard Horner announced a reduction in tolls and by the end of 1810 heavy goods carried between Bath and Newbury could cost £7 by land, a mere £2 7s. by water.

People were not forgotten and at both Bath and Bristol the tradition of passenger-carrying was still in vogue. John Andras' packet boat had been plying the navigable stretches of canal east of Bath since the early 1800s as had a rival craft owned by a Mr Guy of Chippenham. The latter enterprise was seemingly not as successful (or, more likely, did not, unlike Andras', operate under the patronage of the Kennet & Avon Canal Company) and Andras was given authority by the company to purchase the craft 'if it can be got on reasonable terms'. Andras' boat was used for the K&ACC's tour of inspection of the works west of Devizes in July 1808 and subsequently described by the *Bath Chronicle* as an 'elegant packet boat'. In June 1810 he gave notice to the public that 'the canal from BRADFORD-ON-AVON to BATH was opened on WEDNESDAY June 27 and the PLEASURE and PACKET BOATS will start, with their approved accommodations, and usual regularity on MONDAY July 3rd'. At Bristol, Lewis & Thomas (whose wharf along the Back – later known as Welsh Back – was used by other carriers such as Messrs. Haines, Wilson & Gerring, Britton's and Richard Horner) were operating a steam-boat to Bath – quite a technological innovation for 1814. *Charlotte* (perhaps so-called after Symington's pioneering steam tug, the *Charlotte Dundas*) was a Bath and Bristol packet doing a trip each way every weekday – Monday, Wednesday and Friday to Bath; Tuesday, Thursday and Saturday back to Bristol – and by March 1814 was plying between Bristol and Bath every day. Lewis-less, Charles Thomas continued running his 'Avon Packet Boat' (the *Charlotte* had proved unsuccesful on the river and was soon replaced) into the 1820s, by which time he had reverted to the one-trip-a-day timetable.

Clearly it made sense for passenger-carrying craft to operate in sections of the navigation where there were few or no locks; unlike goods, people could get out and circumvent such obstacles in a fraction of the time it would take for a boat to work through. That said, there is no evidence that, after the initial euphoria had abated, the Bristol–London link as such was ever exploited to any great extent, despite the lure of the 'without Shifting' advertisements and Euclid Shaw's 1825 claim that his craft could ply between Bristol and London in five days – one less than his rivals (who, incidentally, soon followed suit and knocked a day off their running time . . . though, unlike Euclid, none claimed to be 'water carriers to His Majesty'). Indeed in 1814 less than 30% of the lucrative trade in manufacturing goods and raw materials was carried the whole length of the waterway. The fact that much of the goods traffic was, like the carrying of passengers, locally based is not really surprising given the distances involved and the number of locks. Nevertheless, whatever the distance, speed was of the essence as evidenced by the appearance in 1814 of so-called 'fly boats' operated by Messrs. Haines, Wilson & Gerring (later just Haines). As this company specialised in trade between Bristol and the upper Thames (and thence the Midlands) through the Wilts & Berks Canal (opened in 1810 linking the Kennet & Avon at Semington with the Thames at Abingdon), their craft would have been narrow beamed and clearly faster than the broader and heavier barges. By the late 1820s the concept of the 'fly boat' had been extended to encompass the notion of speed in terms of working virtually non-stop and carriers such as Betts & Drewe were advertising 'fly barges' that were able to 'perform the Passage [between Bristol and London] in Four or Five Days, and all intermediate places in appropriate times – unavoidable detentions excepted'. At the same time J G Ames & Co were carrying to and from the Midlands via the Severn using their fleet of trows based in Bristol . . . though, unlike other trow owners, they set up a direct link with John Salmon's fly boats at Bath and further transhipment to their own craft 'on the canal at Stourport, in three days to Manchester, Liverpool, Staffordshire Potteries, Derby, Nottingham, and Leicester'.

On the canal itself above the Widcombe locks there were three wharves: the first, just north of Top Lock, was the K&A base of the Somersetshire Coal Canal Company, a quarter of a

1734: Stone is loaded onto barges at Ralph Allen's wharf at Bath; in the background is Old Bridge, downstream of which was the Quay. *Bath City Council.*

mile further on was the SCCC's pre-1810 base at Sydney Wharf while just beyond Sydney Gardens was the smaller Darlington Wharf. These last two saw the coming and going of a considerable number of carriers and 'bargemen', among them Euclid Shaw and Betts & Drewe. Both wharves were basically a cluster of small freestone houses the inhabitants of which invariably seemed to get themselves involved one way or another in the adjacent water-borne trade. Both Euclid Shaw and Aurelius Drewe (Betts dropped out of the partnership during the early 1830s) worked the whole canal from bases in London, Bath and Bristol, though at Bath the former was canal-based while the latter originally operated on the river; the twilight of their years found them both at Sydney Wharf where Aurelius was the K&ACC's 'Traffic Manager' while Euclid was passing over the reins to his sons, James and Thomas.

Assuming these two stalwarts of carrying on the Kennet & Avon were not the bitterest of rivals, the wharfside buildings may well have echoed to many a boatman's tall tale. Did Aurelius embroider his experience at Netham Mill, where there was no towpath, and his resulting 'words' with the Bristol Dock Committee over this deficiency? Perhaps both had

1829: The entrance to the Kennet & Avon Canal at Widcombe, the site of Ralph Allen's stone wharf is in the foreground. *Maurice Scott Collection.*

come close to losing barges here where the combination of wind, current and lack of towpath could be disastrous . . . perhaps, too, both resented the delays and the need to hire 'hoblers' at 5s a time to ensure a safe passage. And Euclid . . . did he bore the breeches off Aurelius with his Royal connections? And just how did these two ageing mariners cope with the Peacock family and their various carrying enterprises from the wharf . . . and with Mary when she became head of the household and was running daily fly boats between Bristol and Devizes?

At Bradford-on-Avon there were two wharves, one (Lower) below the lock and one (Frome Road) above. Both Aurelius and Euclid had agents here too but this was the domain of, among others, two local men, Ebenezer Chapman and Isaac Edmunds. Ebenezer oversaw the wharfside activity above the lock – where there was a gauging dock for the calculation of tolls – on behalf of the K&ACC while Isaac and his family built boats at the lower wharf and ran the ale-house that was eventually to become the Canal Tavern. As the 1840s drew their first eager breath, did these four old hands sniff the smell of steam in the air and realise then that the euphoria had been short-lived and that the light was about to dim on their chosen way of life?

1842: Messrs Packer & Kiver's advert for their 'Scotch' boat service to the Claverton Hotel at Dundas . . . albeit with a modicum of poetic licence as the boat from Bath would not have crossed the aqueduct. *Tim Wheeldon Collection.*

The writing had been on the wall for almost a decade. In 1832 Brunel was doing sterling work; on the one hand, to improve the silting problems of Bristol's Floating Harbour and on the other, overseeing a project that was ultimately to result in the demise of inland water-borne carrying. Like the Canal Age, the Railway Age evolved dramatically, its coming heralded the more boisterously by the allure of its technology. Thomas Gray's *Observations on a General Iron Railway* was published in 1820, a mere five years before the first public railway was opened between Stockton and Darlington. This was a time of accelerating

1840: The regular 'Scotch' boat service races towards Bradford-on-Avon. *Kennet & Avon Canal Trust Collection.*

technical development and thus the K&ACC's achievement and glory was destined to be short-lived as the railways spread their iron tentacles across the land . . . time the only unknown in the inevitability of a Bristol–London link. At Bristol itself things would have been seen somewhat differently; the coming of the Railways could only but serve to enhance the city's reputation and its trading prospects – particularly through the Floating Harbour which, though the tide may have turned, had thus far not brought the increase in trade and prestige envisaged.

For the K&ACC the threat was more real. They had seen it coming as early as 1825 but reconnaissance in the northern territories only served to feed an understandable naivety. At the time their envoy, the engineer John Blackwell, did not espy anything of threatening import to the Kennet & Avon's future. Nevertheless, it was the fear of railway competition that, in 1833, spurred four canal companies, including the K&ACC, to become involved in experiments to find a suitably fast canal craft. These were held on the Oxford Canal, the star attraction being the wrought iron boat *Swallow* which had made the journey from Scotland via Bath. Notwithstanding its impressive statistics over the measured mile and a half at Barby Fields, en route from Bath, on the summit level of the Wilts & Berks Canal, 'she went at two intervals 1560 yards in *four* minutes, and 836 yards in *two* minutes and *twenty eight* seconds.

At these high velocities no injury was done to the banks of the canal . . .'. *Swallow's* ability to attain speeds upwards of 11½mph assured it of a future on the Kennet & Avon and it returned to Bath, the first of several 'Scotch' boats to ply between here and Bradford-on-Avon's Lower Wharf . . . a future, that is, until, under Great Western Railway ownership, the speed limit along the canal was reduced to 4mph!

By the late 1830s the Railway Age was an unavoidable fact, an Act promoting a Bristol–London line via Bath having been passed in 1835. The works actually involved the re-routing of the canal east of Sydney Gardens and, ironically, brought considerable trade to it with the carrying of construction materials for the railway. With due ceremony the Bath–Bristol section opened in August 1840 . . . who among those that gloried in the event, and the subsequent completion of the through route to London the following June, would have thought that in a little over a decade the same Great Western Railway Company would have become the unlikely owners of the Kennet & Avon?

From the Canal Company's point of view it was a spirited and dispiriting decade. They tried to compete by initiating a new twice-weekly fly boat service between London and Bristol in 1843 . . . it ran for less than two years; they reduced tolls in 1841 and 1845 . . . trade increased but toll income continued to fall. In 1846, almost in desperation, they decided to build their own railway – the London, Newbury & Bath Direct Railway – alongside the canal . . . but were outflanked by a GWR-sponsored alternative, the Berks & Hants Railway; they entered the carrying business themselves in 1848 (Aurelius Drewe being the Traffic Manager based at Sydney Wharf) and invested in a 33-vessel fleet that included trows . . . but trade and receipts continued to fall. Finally, beaten by the competitive onslaught of the Age of Steam, the K&ACC offered the canal to the GWR in March 1851; by June 30th, 1852, the formalities complete, the transfer was enacted.

The camera's curious eye recorded none of this.

At his home, Lacock Abbey, close to the Wilts & Berks Canal and even closer to the Avon, Fox Talbot spend much of the 1830s experimenting with the new science of photography and by 1835 had produced his first negatives. Ten years later the camera and the printed image, while out of their infancy, were still at an early stage and did not blossom, either in terms of quality or quantity, until the 1850s. Thus the photographic record of the Kennet & Avon is necessarily that of a waterway in decline, a trading artery already operating in the steamy shadow of an uncompromising rival. Enthusiasts of this new art form devoted more time to capturing the more vibrant sights of an ever-changing Victorian landscape.

And there is, perhaps, one other factor in the dearth of photographic testimony to even the decline of traffic on the Kennet & Avon at work – its aesthetic quality. It is curious how, of the many photographs that exist of Bath's Broad Quay, so few contain a boat. Were there never boats there at the same time as the budding photographer . . . or did the roving eye deliberately avoid the commonplace nature of the people and craft that worked the navigation? Was waterside landscape more visually pleasing than waterside activity?

We shall never know what was just 'out of the picture' nor can all the facets of any location's past be understood or explained. Nevertheless, much can be deduced from other contemporary evidence; people and places can be brought to life, their watery alliance given substance to become, in the eye of the beholder at least, more than mere images of the Kennet & Avon.

HOW THE PHOTOGRAPHS ARE ORDERED

Broadly speaking, the 109 photographs that follow are in linear geographic order starting at Bristol's Floating Harbour and ending at Bradford-on-Avon. Within each general area they are arranged in chronological order; there are a few exceptions where it has clearly made more sense to over-ride the aforementioned logic.

Though a particular photograph may have been taken in, say, the 1930s, the attendant caption might well contain additional information on the location's history as far back as the embryonic days of the navigation – facts and figures, people and places, anecdotes and speculation that, due to the non-existence of contemporary photographic evidence, might otherwise go unrecorded in a book such as this. A similar philosophy lies behind the inclusion of some photographs that might appear, at first glance, to have a low interest factor.

1 A lone square-rigged trow heads towards Bristol Bridge. It probably tied up along the Back (later Welsh Back) although occasionally these craft dropped their masts and rigging and worked their way up to Bath and even – as evidenced by photo 79 – onto the canal. The trow (pronounced to rhyme with 'crow') in its various forms was the indigenous craft of the Severn, its estuary and, from the late 18th century, limited stretches of its connecting canals. Earlier in the century, Ames & Co were the only Bristol-based trow owners who indulged in regular trade to Bath and though small trows were actually made on the Kennet & Avon at Honey Street and Bath, the canal, with its many locks and overbridges, was not its natural environment. c 1877. *PBA*

2 Countless tall masts oversee an inner-Harbour scene of bustling activity. Clearly many of the ships that tied up along these quay walls discharged their cargo both land- and water-wards; in the case of the latter, goods were loaded into barges for transhipment to anywhere as close as another of the Harbour's wharves or as far as Bath or beyond. With the coming of the railway in the early 1840s the extremities of that 'beyond' had been increasingly drawn in closer to Bristol and, as the century drew to a close, rarely extended beyond the man-made barrier of the 29 locks at Devizes. At this time barges travelled round the Harbour using hands, shafts, 'hoblers' and, if lucky, a 'snatch' from a steam tug. The hobler earned a living by touting for business from rowing boats and would tow barges as far as Netham where horses could be hired for the journey up-river. c1860

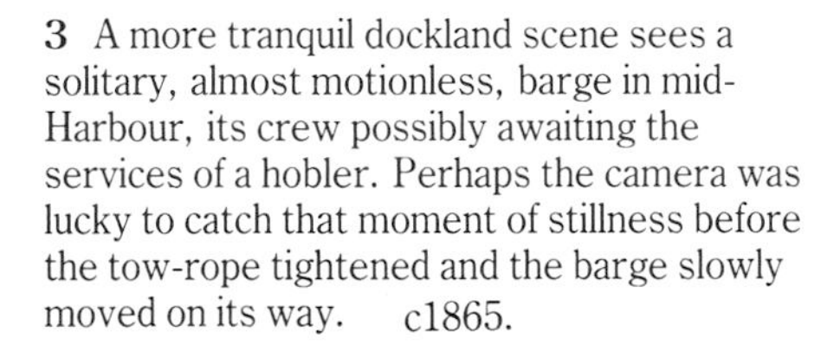

3 A more tranquil dockland scene sees a solitary, almost motionless, barge in mid-Harbour, its crew possibly awaiting the services of a hobler. Perhaps the camera was lucky to catch that moment of stillness before the tow-rope tightened and the barge slowly moved on its way. c1865.

4 This late 19th century view of Bush Corner (today's Arnolfini) espies a port in a state of transition. The truncated St Augustine's Reach plays host to both the new order and the old; steam and sail rub shoulders in short-lived harmony. Scavenger-like barges load up for the next stage of the transhipment process to . . . well, not very far; of the 195,000 tons that was moved inland along the Feeder Canal and through Netham in 1905, less than 27,000 tons got as far as Hanham Lock and the waters of the Kennet & Avon and only 1,100 tons of that actually found its way onto the canal itself east of Bath. c1895. *PBA*

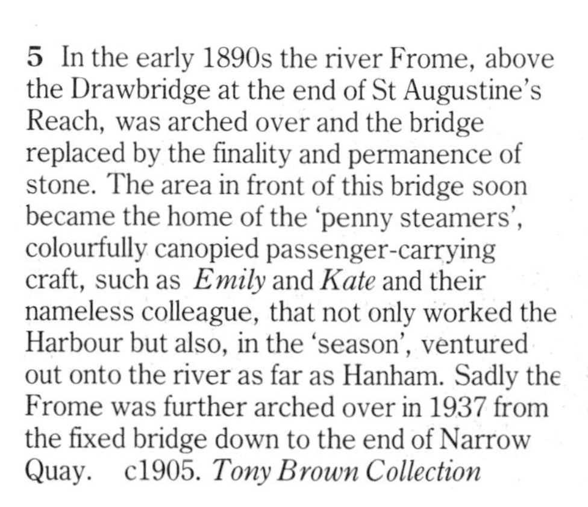

5 In the early 1890s the river Frome, above the Drawbridge at the end of St Augustine's Reach, was arched over and the bridge replaced by the finality and permanence of stone. The area in front of this bridge soon became the home of the 'penny steamers', colourfully canopied passenger-carrying craft, such as *Emily* and *Kate* and their nameless colleague, that not only worked the Harbour but also, in the 'season', ventured out onto the river as far as Hanham. Sadly the Frome was further arched over in 1937 from the fixed bridge down to the end of Narrow Quay. c1905. *Tony Brown Collection*

6 & 7 From the late 19th century the area by the ferry steps between Bristol Bridge and the Back was a favourite spot for the laying up of light barges or loaded barges – particularly those belonging to United Alkali (later ICI) – awaiting a tug or a 'snatch' up to Netham. The opening of the Kennet & Avon brought in its wake a glut of carriers, many of whom advertised their services from specific wharf-side bases; most of these were within a few hundred yards of Bristol Bridge along the Back, Redcliffe Back, Temple Back and Counterslip. But by the turn of the century, when these picture-postcard views were taken, few barge owners had their own water-side base as such, though exceptions included Gerrish & Co, who regularly plied to Bath and beyond from a wharf along Redcliffe Street, and the Midland Railway which had a wharf near Temple Meads Arches. c1905.
Tony Brown and Chris Gibson Collections

8 By the mid-1920s the age of sail was but a memory. Barrels of paraffin wax are being unloaded from the Bristol City Line's *New York City* – tied up alongside Z shed at Canon's Marsh – into barges probably bound for the Polysulphin works at Keynsham while a steam tug passes by with a light barge in tow. 1926. *PBA*

9 The barge traffic along the Feeder Canal and the river Avon was, of course, two-way – though undoubtedly the major part was *from* the City Docks rather than *to* it. That said, the barges photographed here are unloading their cargo of galvanised iron sheets – manufactured at the Lysaghts works by the Feeder Canal – onto a Coast Line steamer near the Grove Shed. A Mr Brown operated a pair of narrow boats under contract from Coast Line to carry raw materials to Polysulphin at Keynsham; when Brown died, George Head – see caption 18 – took over the contract using barges. 1927. *PBA*

10 No 1 Shed on Broad Quay was also known as the Dublin Shed, but the bargemen taking on wood-pulp from the *Stalheim* would certainly have known it by its nickname, the 'Guiness' shed. Fred Ashmead & Son's pulp-laden barges, the *Cressy* and the *Avon,* would probably have been towed by the tug *Conroy* to the St Anne's Board Mills on the Avon just upstream of Netham. 1929. *PBA*

11 The view from Colston Avenue takes in the Tramway Centre and puts Broad and Narrow Quays into their inner-city context. In the middle distance another steam-tug, possibly Ashmead's *Hubert*, manoeuvres in front of E Shed, nowadays better known as the Watershed. 1929. *PBA*

12 Berthed at Broad Quay, the *Star* discharges wood-pulp into one of Fred Ashmead & Son's distinctive Honey Street barges, the *Hopeful*. Though built on the Kennet & Avon, such barges seldom returned to the canal of their birth; indeed the dimensions of some were such that it was only with great difficulty that they actually got through the 44 canal locks onto the Avon in the first place. In 1898 a newly-built barge, probably the *Harriet*, bound for Ashmeads damaged one of the Devizes locks, the event being reported to the Canal Committee by the builders, Robbins & Co of Honey Street, thus, '. . . in order to effect passage of a vessel of exceptional structure and dimensions through a lock at Foxhangers [they] had chipped portions off the wooden quoins and the brickwork at the sides of the lock.' c1930. *PBA*

13 A closer look at the bales of wood-pulp that, though normally destined for St Annes, did occasionally (about one barge-load in 50) find their way further up-river to the paper mills at Keynsham. The tug and all the barges belonged to Fred Ashmead & Son, carriers from as far back as the 1840s when most of their business was conducted from the Beehive public house at Crew's Hole. At this time it was not unknown for their fly boats to work across the Kennet & Avon to Reading, head up the Thames to Inglesham, westwards through the Thames & Severn and Stroudwater Canals and back down to Bristol via the Severn. In the early part of the 20th century Ashmeads carried sand and gravel in trows from Appledore in Devon to Welsh Back for transfer to barges and thence to Keynsham or Bath. c1930. *PBA*

14 The end of another day for two of Ashmead's men at Bush Corner. Aboard the *Hubert*, Bill Jones checks his trusty bike. Bill took his bike everywhere; it was his trademark not least because it had the habit of getting entangled with the ropes. On one occasion his 'mates' blacked out his headlamp so that he thought his battery had gone flat. c1950. *Hubert Ashmead*

15 The steam-tug, *Cress*, pulls one of ICI's 'precious stones', the barge *Onyx*, past Bathurst Wharf en route to their Netham works during the early 1930s. Three bargemen (two of whom were the brothers, George and Sam Smith, photographed here) worked almost the entire fleet of dumb barges which carried mostly soda ash and chemicals to and from Netham; indeed so adept were these three at trimming the barges that when anyone else tried to do so they invariably got it wrong and took in water. ICI hired tugs – *Cress* was one of Ashmead's – as and when necessary. In the background one of the Dock authority's mud barges, probably the *Axe* or the *Kenn*, heads towards Underfall Yard with its cargo of dredgings from the Feeder Canal. c1932. *PBA*

16 Accidents do happen . . . as the crew of this pulp-laden barge, the *Celtic* – another of Ashmead's Honey Street barges – discovered in Bathurst Basin. But help was at hand in the shape of a steam crane and the friendly form of the tug, *Hubert*. . . wherever there was an Ashmead barge neither the *Hubert* nor the *Conroy* was likely to be far away. The latter actually came to Bristol from London via the Kennet & Avon Canal in the spring of 1929; being 52ft long with a beam of 12ft, its dimensions presented no problems . . . but the 5ft 6in draught was a different story. In its prime the canal could hardly have coped: in its death-throes it only just did, the *Conroy*'s draught having been reduced to a mere 3ft by removing everything including the engine and boiler. c1950. *Hubert Ashmead*

17 *Conroy* tows a line of barges – the first of which is loaded with wood-pulp for St Annes – between Welsh and Redcliffe Backs. Buchanan's Warehouse – originally Baker's granary and mill built in the early 1880s – is on the right at the northern end of Redcliffe Back. Back in the early 19th century there were several wharves between here and Bristol Bridge that backed onto Redcliffe Street; two of these, Bull and Dundas, specialised in trade to Bath and beyond. The former became Euclid Shaw's Bristol base in the early 1820s while the latter was Thomas Jordan's (originally Baker, Jordan & Co) until he moved across the water to William Terrell's wharf at 33 Back. Dundas Wharf was probably also the Bristol base of carriers C & R Parker, Daniel Phipp and Gerrish & Co, all of whom used a Redcliffe Back/Redcliffe Street address and were successive carriers from Bath's Kingston Wharf from 1830 until the early 1900s. Gerrish & Co claimed that 'Goods delivered . . . in Bristol by 5pm arrive in Bath 7am next morning, and are delivered forthwith.'

Terrell's was one of two wharves on the Back that had strong river and canal connections; the other, Charles Thomas', was used by several carriers up to and beyond the decline in traffic during the 1840s – only then did Thomas' packet boat cease to honour its daily round trip to Bath. These two were also rivals when it came to trade with the Wilts & Berks Canal; for many years their wharves played host to Messrs Saunders and Hopkins, both of whom operated twice-weekly fly boats to and from Abingdon.
c1950. *Hubert Ashmead*

18 Albert Head, who, with his brother George, ran a small carrying business from the 1920s, watches from his timber-laden barge, the *Rose*, as one of William Butler & Co's barges, the *Darby*, heads for Crew's Hole. The crane in the background is on Dundas Wharf which, as its name suggests, once had such close connections with the traffic up-river to Bath. The *Darby*'s barrels of pitch or resin are almost matched by its human cargo – the latter probably Butler employees taking advantage of a lift back to Crew's Hole at the end of a hard day's work.

The Head brothers often tied up along Welsh Back while one or the other (usually George) nipped ashore to call in at their Queen Square office. It was back at the beginning of the century that their father, George, first took on some work for timber merchants Taylor & Lowe, having been 'hijacked' by the former on his daily trip across the Harbour on the Mardyke ferry which George ran. In addition to carrying – mostly timber in those days – George supplied Taylor & Lowe and others with barges for use as stages between the shallow-water timber berths and vessels unloading.
c1930. *PBA*

19 The barges first seen in photograph 17 have moved on beyond Bristol Bridge and, having encountered one of the Port's mud barges, are passing between the Castle grounds and George's (later Courage's) Brewery. It has been said that the last 'narrow boat' to work these waters, the *Halfren*, regularly unloaded at the hoist halfway along the Brewery's water-frontage . . . and even that it used the Kennet & Avon Canal to bring in the hops all the way from Kent!

The *Halfren*, usually skippered by Jack Plumpton, whose father owned Beese's Tea Gardens, was indeed a frequent user of George's hoist but its cargo was normally malt brought, not from Kent, but from a small wharf by the Temple Meads arches . . . a mere 500 yards away. And, though it was a narrower boat, it had a 10ft beam, was double-ended and was, unusually, owned by Benjamin Perry's – shippers mainly involved with the tobacco trade, since the 1860s. Up to the 1940s, malt was also brought down to George's from Bath by, among others, Francis & Niblett's (Bathavon Transport from October 1941) *Avon King* and *Avon Queen*. The railed craft on the left is the *Kingstonian*, a passenger-carrying boat owned and run by Albert Head.
c1950. *Hubert Ashmead*

20 Albert Head's *Kingstonian* sweeps round from Bristol Bridge en route to Keynsham. In the background one of Silvey & Co's boats, the motor-ship *Safety*, unloads coal brought across from Lydney in the Forest of Dean to, in this case, the Tramway Generating Station, just round the corner from George's Brewery. Silvey's also supplied fuel to St Anne's Board Mills using, in addition to the *Safety*, three erstwhile shallow-keeled trows, the *Willie*, *Yarra* and *George*. The *Kingstonian* started its passenger-carrying life on the river Thames at Kingston. Shortly after the war Albert Head had it brought across to Bristol to compete with Frank Niblett's *River Queen*; by the end of 1948 the latter, which carried only 140 people compared with the *Kingstonian*'s 220, was gone. Albert's brother, George, ran another trip boat, the *Lady Betty* which he had purchased from J Hitchens who had long been operating passenger craft such as the *Sylvia* and the *Flying Fox* both around the Harbour (usually from the Tramway Centre steps) and on the river to Hanham Mills and Keynsham.

The frontage either side of 'Halfpenny' (St Philips) Bridge (from where this photograph was taken) was once bustling with the paraphernalia of wharves, warehouses and barges geared to the trade upriver. Counterslip and Temple Back offered carriers like Aurelius Drewe and, for a time, Euclid Shaw both permanent wharfage and easy access to the Harbour and the city. In 1815 Betts, Burton & Drewe offered to lease water frontage from the Dock Committee 'to facilitate docks, sheds etc' on which they expected to have to spend £300 over and above their rent of £15 per annum for 21 years. It seems that their bid was unsuccessful for a few years later they took over Thomas Parson's Kennet Wharf (sited between the entrance to the Castle moat and the bridge) and renamed it Queen Street.
c1950. *Albert Head*

21 It may seem strange to see boats bearing the name of a railway company but for the Midland there were distinct advantages in using the river and canal to link with their depots at Bristol and Bath. From the late 19th century the company's fleet of red-painted barges, based here at Avonside Wharf on the Bristol Bridge side of Temple Meads arches, carried goods from the Harbour for transfer to railway waggons. The waggon on the left of the photograph bears the name of Wm Butler & Co whose products were frequently carried here by barge from Crew's Hole for transhipment.

In 1896–97 the Midland Railway purchased another wharf, King's, in front of the Redcliffe caves, enlarged its barge fleet and acquired the steam tug pictured here. Early the next century they sold their barge fleet to Benjamin Perry & Son and George Head (Snr) subsequently acquired two by doing a 'swap' with a converted schooner, the *Kathleen Ellen*. Across the water from Avonside the rival GWR also had a wharf from about the late 1870s; this in turn replaced a barge dock built as early as 1840 which, ironically, probably played its part in the carrying of materials for the building of the railway to Bath. 1922. *National Railway Museum/Kennet & Avon Canal Trust Collection*

22 The narrow jaws that were the gateway from the Floating Harbour to Totterdown Basin and the Feeder Canal were overseen from 1821 by Bristol Gas Light Company's (later the Bristol United Gas Light Company, then British Gas) Avon Street complex. During the late 1940s Welsh coal was still being brought direct to the works on small coastal vessels; from round the corner on the Feeder the unwanted tar from the gas-making process was taken to Butlers at Crew's Hole in the *Carbolate, Jolly* and *Darby*; until February 1967 the last two also brought tar down from Bath's riverside Gas Works, the last regular commercial traffic on the Avon.

Another by-product of the gas works at Canon's Marsh, gas water, was carried to the Avon Street works by Ashmead's barges. Some of the waterside coke heaps along the Feeder Canal had a tendency to slide, little by little, into the water but, as coke floats, it was retrievable. It is said that one duo assigned to this task in a rowing boat tackled the job with so much zeal that they overfilled the boat . . . and it sank!

Those who worked the barges remember this corner for other reasons: when water was being flushed through into the Harbour from Netham Lock, a tug towing a line of barges could itself make the turn but its retinue invariably went straight on to end up as an ignominious pile-up by the entrance to the old Totterdown Lock, the erstwhile link with the New Cut. In 1872 Bristol and Bath carriers, Gerrish & Sainsbury, took the Docks Committee to court claiming compensation for loss of trade caused through the practice of letting off water from the upper part of the Floating Harbour.
1949. *Brian Milsom Collection*

23 The *Conroy* pulls its line of barges along the Feeder Canal towards Netham Lock. In the left background is the massive edifice of the Great Western Cotton Works built in 1838 and fuelled with coal from barges and trows plying the Feeder; ashes and clinker for road works were taken by barge up-river from the 'Cotton Factory' to Swineford and Keynsham and even as far as Sydney Wharf on the canal. The tightly terraced houses that once looked up to the mill's stone and brick facade, though more characterful than the concrete alternatives of the 1960s, were in an area that had embraced all the worst aspects of Victorian industry. In 1874 the *Bristol Mercury* described the environs of the Feeder Canal thus: '. . . the chosen home of the manure manufacturies, bone-crushing mills, knacker yards, horseflesh-boiling factories, and works which in the manufacture of chemical products throw off nauseous gases, causing stench-laden folds of air to envelope the visitor and make him involuntarily turn to the water side to try if he can breathe more freely.'

If nothing else, the Feeder Canal itself seemed a friendlier place, though not so for one child who, in 1876, slipped on the wooden edge to the towpath made wet by the wash of passing barges, fell in and drowned. Many of the 154 barges carrying cargo within the Floating Harbour at the time would also have navigated the Feeder; none would have had any respect for the niceties of watching their wash!

On the left of the line of barges is the disused entrance to the Feeder Cut, built originally as a through route for river traffic via the New Cut while the Feeder was being constructed. In 1871 'several Barge owners and Millers . . . between the cities of Bristol and Bath' asked the Docks Committee to restore it on the grounds that '. . . it would much facilitate Trade by enabling Barges to proceed direct from these Docks into the River Avon above the Feeder and thereby avoiding the Port of Bristol and effecting a considerable saving in time and expense.' Their representations fell on deaf ears. c1950. *Hubert Ashmead*

24 Two of Ashmead's boats, the barge *Orion* and the motor-ship *Beauleigh*, lie outside Netham Lock. The latter was built at Charles Hill's and could get through Netham with its cargo of coal for the Board Mills only by taking down its mast, funnel and wheelhouse. The small hut at the tail of the lock (see also photograph 23) was Ashmead's post-1931 office outside which the 'under-the-lamp' men used to gather at 8 o'clock each morning in the hope of some casual work.

At Netham, in the days of horse-drawn boats, horses could be hired for the haul up-river, the last such suppliers being Bill Kendall of Conham Hill and James Meredith of the Lower Bristol Road, Bath. Whenever the horses arrived at their destination they simply turned round and walked back home; it is said that Meredith's horses would even walk down from Bath to Netham ready for an 8 o'clock start. How, or even if, these self-reliant horses coped with the three horse-ferries en route remains their secret!

It seems that when Frank Niblett and Bill Francis first went into the carrying business in the mid 1930s they often had trouble finding a horse here for their pair of narrow boats, the suspicion being that a rival carrier had 'arranged' the inconvenience. Ironically it was through this local difficulty that they met Fred Short of Bath who not only had a horse but also a riverside wharf ripe for development. In 1941 this trio was to unite as Bathavon Transport.

A comparison of the traffic through Netham in two months a decade apart is as illuminating as it is puzzling: in May 1937 there were 654 recorded boat movements which carried a total of 5,089 tons (only 461 of which were going *to* Bristol; in May 1947 380 boat movements carried 10,463 tons (974 to Bristol). Half the boats carrying twice the cargo may seem almost contradictory but the war years had a way of concentrating the mind and the upsurge in trade was to be short-lived thanks mainly to the ubiquitous lorry. By May 1967 there were a mere 195 movements all of which were Ashmead barges carrying wood pulp to St Annes . . . all, that is, except the 32 trips made by the Avon Boating Co's *Kingstonian* to Hanham. (In 1953 the *Kingstonian* had been taken to Stourport by the Head brothers – they sold their barges to Ashmeads the same year – where it ran until 1963 when Harry Hoskins bought it and brought it back to Bristol.)
c1952 *Hubert Ashmead*

25 Part of ICI's fleet of mostly Honey Street barges lies tied up at their Netham works. The barges were invariably called after precious stones – *Emerald, Jasper, Onyx, Opal, Pearl* and *Ruby* – and, being dumb, required the services of a tug; in the early 1950s the entire fleet (with the exception of *Pearl*, which went into private hands and was finally destroyed by flooding at Keynsham in 1977) was bought up by Ashmeads.

The ICI works stood close to the site of Netham Mill around which there was originally no towpath – even after the rest of the navigation was so endowed. The mill had been occupied by brass manufacturers Anderson, New & Co (later Pitt, Anderson Birch & Co) from the early 1800s and, although the Bristol Dock Company had successfully forced them to vacate the site by 1820, there was still no towpath. This deficiency caused the carriers Betts & Drewe, not only to note that here was '. . . far the most dangerous part of the navigation between this and London' but also, in December 1822, to write to the Docks Committee thus: '. . . at this season of the year it is with great difficulty we can stem the current at this place for want of one [a towing path]. Within the course of the last fortnight, we had nearly lost two valuable Barge loads of Goods at that place, by being overpowered by the wind and current, and had not the anchor held fast, and the Rope good, one of them would have been totally lost. The Anchor of the other was drifted a considerable distance before it fastened, had it not, that also must have shared the same fate. Independent of the risk, it costs us on the average five shillings per Barge for hired men or Hoblers (who live in this, or plunder) to pass the Mill, and a delay from one to two hours.' c1940. *John Cornwell Collection*

26 Both geographically and historically, Crew's Hole (Screw's Hole on some early maps) was the last outpost of Bristol's riverside industry. It was also one of the earliest being, from the 1750s, the site of brass and copper works. Brunel's need for creosote helped establish a tar distillery which was managed by William Butler from 1843; Butler bought the works after a disastrous fire in 1863 thus establishing the firm of William Butler & Co. As the same company had a similar site at Upper Parting on the river Severn at Gloucester, water transport played an important part in Butler's business of processing the tar into by-products such as pitch, creosote and benzole. Over the years Butlers utilised almost every form of water transport from horse-drawn long boats (so-called narrow boats were more commonly called 'long' on the Severn and the lower reaches of the Avon) with tanks capable of carrying 40 tons to sailing trows which carried pitch from Crew's Hole to the South Wales ports and returned with coal. This group of Butler employees is probably posing for the camera on the steam-tug *Irene* which helped bridge the gap between horse-drawn and self-propelled barges. One of the company's trows is in the background; these were phased out during and after the Great War having become, in terms of time and wages, totally uneconomical. c1902. *John Cornwell Collection*

27 There has always been a member of the Sweet family working for Butlers. Charles Sweet used to work his boats, *Endeavour, Ada* and *Adelaide* to Bath, Bradford-on-Avon, Trowbridge, Devizes and even Newbury to collect tar and was often away from his native Bristol for a week or more. His son, Jim, was thus brought up to the ways of the river and the tar trade and not surprisingly followed in Charles' footsteps. Jim is seen here (second from right) on the *Carbolate* along with William Stiff (right) and Stanley White (extreme left), father to Felix White who later skippered the *Darby* (see caption 34), at the Crew's Hole works. Crew's Hole also supported another small carrier in the late 1880s; W H Pearce traded in stone, coal, coke and sand with his horse-drawn narrow boat, *Eviline*. c1920. *James Cole Collection*

28 The *Carbolate*, twin-screwed with two economical twin-cylinder Brit engines, was built in 1911, its six tanks having a total capacity of 120 tons. It normally carried liquids between Crew's Hole and Gloucester via the Avon, Severn and Gloucester & Sharpness Canal. The *Carbolate* is pictured here at Crew's Hole; behind is the barge *Isabelle* which used to bring tar down-river from Bath's Gas Works. In the background is what was reputedly the first iron barge ever built, the *Alexander*. The *'Alec'* was bought second-hand by Butlers and people, sceptical of the floating properties of iron, used to come from miles around to see it. Successive generations were not disappointed for *'Alec'* remained afloat for over 100 years, ending its days as a storage barge.
c1920. *James Cole Collection*

29 Established in 1846 on this riverside site opposite Conham Vale, Beese's Tea Gardens soon became a popular venue for local pleasure boats and walkers via the ancient Conham Ferry. On Bank Holidays, a barge was often fixed broadside across the river as a 'permanent' ferry. Just upriver was Hanham Colliery Wharf from where coal was barged by Fred Martin & Son to the Feeder Road Power Station in *Rose, Tyre* and *Lizzie*. These last two were Honey Street barges and *Tyre*, renamed *Celtic* by Ashmeads, sank in Bathurst Basin – see photograph 16. The Colliery itself ran two barges, *Irene* and *Ann*, largely engaged in bunkering the dock's dredging flotilla.
c1910. *James Cole Collection*

30 Hanham Mills was, until the late 1720s, the limit of navigation east from Bristol. With the construction of the Avon Navigation, Hanham Lock effectively became the border between the Navigation Company's (later the GWR's) territory and that of Bristol Corporation (later the Port of Bristol). Hanham Lock and weir had another claim to fame in that, curiously, the horse towing path went round the weir side and not alongside the lock. The crew of the barge *Maria* is using a shaft to leave the lock before using the river's downstream flow to pick up the horse on the far bank. The lowered 'mast' is a derrick used for loading and unloading cargo – see also photographs 31 and 32. During the last war, the Head family moored their unique floating air-raid shelter, the converted ex-fire float *Salamander*, at the tail of the lock . . . perhaps Albert and George, like many of the other working boatmen at the time, remembered the welcoming smile of the keeper here, Mrs Taylor, her cups of tea and home-made cake. c1910. *Kennet & Avon Canal Trust Collection*

31 Why these two Honey Street barges, apparently crewless, should be tied up below the weir here is unknown, though there would seem to be several possibilities. In the centre background the small building and derrick on the left bank locate the riverside wharf next to Fox's Wood Quarry. The stone from this quarry was reputedly better than that from other local quarries – John Rennie recommended that stone from here be used on the quoins of the Devizes locks – and, even though the river was particularly narrow here, the wharf was kept busy. Perhaps this pair of barges has laid up by the weir to await their turn at the wharf, their crew having crossed the river via the ferry to the old Chequers. The other possibility is that the lock is busy (see photograph 32) and the barges' crew is waiting for clear access to it before dropping the boats back, round the island's tongue head, and into the lock. Meanwhile the horse has probably gone off to graze having been 'dropped' somewhere round the site of the ruins of Hanham Mill itself. c1902. *John Cornwell Collection*

32 For those working the river the lock was just another toll point, its keeper being authorised to extract the necessary lockage dues. As early as 1729 the proprietors of the Navigation prohibited their lock-keepers from selling liquor other than ale; but here at least there was some compensation . . . the well (see photograph 30) by the keeper's cottage was renowned locally for the cool sweetness of its water and few could resist partaking. Perhaps that is why, contrary to the popular image of competitive conflict between rival working boatmen, there seems to be little sense of urgency in this confrontation between a pair of narrow boats and a barge at Hanham. Perhaps these two are not rivals at all (Henry Gerrish, for example, ran both narrow boats and barges), though the odds are that the narrow boats are J & J Noad's pair that regularly carried 50 tons of grain from Avonmouth to their mill at Littleton near Semington while the empty barge could belong to its builders, Robbins, Lane & Pinniger, who frequently brought timber to Honey Street from Avonmouth at the time. In 1931 the former's narrow boats were taken over by Bristol-based Francis & Niblett and three years later the same carriers also took on the timber run on behalf of Robbins, Lane & Pinniger.
c1902. *John Cornwell Collection*

33 Mother and child await the ferry . . . or do they? Certainly there was a ferry across the river here (just upstream of Hanham Lock and weir) but this picture-postcard view is just one of a series for which the unknown lady and child posed. Hanham was one of several ferries across the river between Bristol and Bath; there were two downstream at St Annes and Conham and others upstream, including three that carried horses across the river where the towpath changed sides. Perhaps the unknown pair did make it across to the old Chequers (now the Old Lock & Weir) but sadly they don't seem to have posed by the site of the cockpit behind the pub where, so the story goes, men from the barges and the local quarries would wager away many a florin . . . and sometimes finish off with a good brawl. c1902.

34 The original Chequers Inn is photographed here alongside its more modern namesake. During the late 1940s the old Chequers was a private residence, the home of the Blackwell family who ran a boat-building and repair yard specialising in pleasure craft. The occasion was the Cabot Cruising Club's regatta to which Frank Niblett's steam trip-boat, the *River Queen* (on the left) had been invited. The *River Queen* was put out of business by Albert Head's larger rival, the *Kingstonian* (see caption 20). Blackwells built the wheelhouses for William Butler's *Jolly* and *Darby*; Felix White, the skipper of the latter, would often drop off a barrel of tar, an essential ingredient in the boat-building business.
1948. *Bob Blackwell Collection*

35 Blackwells converted a number of ex-working narrow boats for pleasure use. One of these, *Queen*, was brought from Newbury via the canal and river for a local artist, Percy de Ballance. In 1950 Ballance took some seven weeks to get *Queen* to Hungerford and a further three weeks to return to Hanham. His was one of the last attempts at navigating a canal already fast deteriorating, a canal on which carrying had all but ceased.
1950. *Bob Blackwell Collection*

36 Londonderry Wharf is one of two Avon & Gloucestershire Railway wharves either side of Keynsham Lock (the other being Avon) that once provided outlets onto the Avon for coal from the Gloucestershire collieries at Mangotsfield and Coalpit Heath. From the early 1830s coal was transported along a single track, standard gauge line in waggons pulled by horses with some assistance from gravity, a system that, a little over a decade later, literally got caught up in the advance of the Railway Age in general and the Bristol & Gloucester Railway in particular.

The Kennet & Avon Canal Company had a financial stake in the A&GR but were unable to stave off the inevitable pressure from the railways and especially the B&GR's new owners, the Midland Railway. The K&ACC itself was taken over by the GWR in 1852 and within 15 years the A&GR and its wharves were all but inactive. During the 1880s, however, the line was re-opened to accommodate coal from the California pit at Oldland but this ceased in 1904 when the pit suffered severe flooding. This photo not only shows the wharfside crane and the store house but also the tiny weigh-house just to the right of the cottage. The chimney in the background belongs to the Polysulphin works (on the other side of Keynsham) which itself lies almost directly opposite Avon Wharf. c1902. *John Cornwell Collection*

37 The name 'Londonderry Wharf' is not one with which the working boatman was generally familiar – mention 'Jack White's Corner' and you're talking the same language. Jack White was a Keynsham lock-keeper and lived in the cottage pictured here behind the towpath bridge over Siston Brook; like many of the keepers on the river he was a memorable character, so much so that his name lingers on locally with his erstwhile abode still bearing his name. Albert and Phyllis Head remember once bringing a Sunday School party here on the *Kingstonian* . . . and recall how, while the children and the poorer parents went off to a nearby field for their picnic, the vicar excluded himself to concentrate on wooing one of the 'pillars' of the Church! c1910.

38 A passenger-carrying steamer – possibly the *Emily* or the *Kate* from Bristol – enters the weir loop alongside Keynsham Lock to turn before heading back down-river. On the lock-side is the keeper's brick-built base, once the snug retreat of Jack White. In the background is the old County Bridge which was swept away in 1968 by the swollen waters of the Avon.
c1920. *Tony Brown Collection*

39 Albert Head's *Kingstonian* has also made it to the tail of Keynsham Lock, its passengers about to disembark and make their way up past the lock, across White Hart Bridge and onto the island beyond the lock-cut where the Heads had their weir-side tea-gardens (see photograph 44).
c1950. *Albert Head*

40 The *Kingstonian* would normally turn below the lock before taking on its passengers for the return trip to Bristol, though in this case it seems to have gone into the lock – much to the annoyance of the local children for whom it was clearly a swimming pool! Albert and Phyllis Head have many cherished memories of running the *Kingstonian* though, as we have seen, there were parties best forgotten. Another such group was a party of under-privileged children whose outing was arranged by a respected religious charity . . . but, for the organisers, charity definitely began at home and their charges were noticeably deprived of any sustenance while they themselves tucked in voraciously. So outraged was Phyllis Head that she quickly made plate-loads of sandwiches for the children . . . and was conveniently booked up when the same charity next wanted to hire the *Kingstonian.* 1950. *Albert Head*

41 Keynsham Lock is dwarfed by the imposing red brick of the Fry's Chocolate Factory, clearly still under construction. Despite its proximity to the river, no facility for exploitation of the navigation was ever envisaged; indeed when Albert Head approached the company during the 1940s with a proposal to bring in some of the raw materials by barge the response was an emphatic 'No!' Perhaps they had witnessed the fun and games when, in the early '30s, one of Francis & Niblett's bargemen, Harry Escott ('Emmer'), lost the *Honer* when it – and its cargo of wheat – sank in Keynsham Lock overnight.

Perhaps too their reasoning was not unconnected with the unpredictable nature of river transport, one aspect of which is also illustrated in this photograph. Either as a result of maintenance work or drought conditions, the short cut upstream of the lock is clearly very low; at other times of the year – as some of the following photographs graphically illustrate – the reverse could be the case. It was just such erratic behaviour that, back in 1809, gave impetus to the notion of a Bath & Bristol Canal to by-pass the river navigation. As can be seen, the gates of the lock have been left open, the normal working practice on the river.
1922. *Chris Gibson Collection*

42 As if to emphasise the point just made about flooding, the barge pictured here is caught in just such conditions below White Hart Bridge. Because of its low haunches the bridge was always difficult to navigate when the river was running high – being further out of the water, light barges, such as the one here, had even greater problems. Albert Head was once towing an empty side-cloth trow down from Bath with the river running fast and high and was determined to get through White Hart before it rose too high. He just made it and tied up the trow on the offside just below the White Hart pub before adjourning to Bristol by bus for the night. Next morning found the trow adrift in the middle of the pub's garden and it was only with great difficulty that he and his mate retrieved it before the waters fell and left it high and dry.   c1915.

43 Under less fraught conditions White Hart Bridge and its attendant hostelry were an altogether more welcoming sight for the working boatman. This photograph shows more clearly the way in which the bridge's stone arch drops away sharply from the keystone and how wider craft might be affected particularly when the river was running high. Despite the fact that the pub's cellars have long harboured a ghostly tale, for the boatman the temptation of its thirst-quenching ale usually over-rode such mundane considerations. c1930. *Tony Brown Collection*

44 Keynsham weir was the picturesque backdrop for Albert Head's tea-gardens, the 'half-way house' that gave the *Kingstonian*'s passengers a chance to stretch their legs and wet their whistles. The weir was originally an integral part of the nearby water-powered Avon Brass Mill, indeed the Avon-side brass industry had rights over and above the right of navigation should the river be running low. In the early days of the river navigation it was not unknown for locks to be closed to allow a head of water to build up for the mills. That said, in the fullness of time water power was superseded by steam, and coal was thus carried by water to some mills. Above the weir was the Keynsham paper mills to which rolls of Scandinavian paper were imported via Bristol and the river. c1950. *Albert Head*

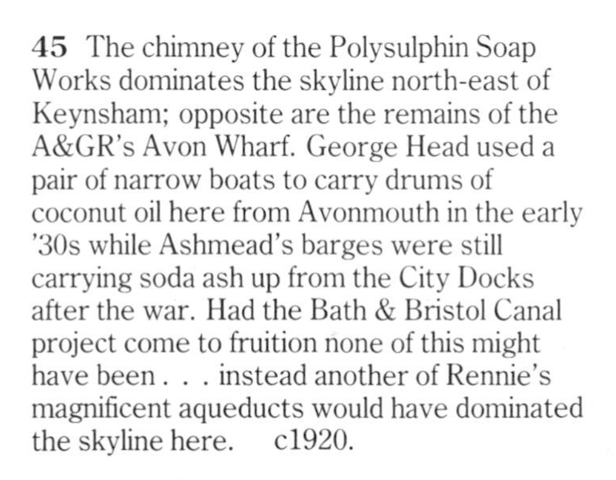

45 The chimney of the Polysulphin Soap Works dominates the skyline north-east of Keynsham; opposite are the remains of the A&GR's Avon Wharf. George Head used a pair of narrow boats to carry drums of coconut oil here from Avonmouth in the early '30s while Ashmead's barges were still carrying soda ash up from the City Docks after the war. Had the Bath & Bristol Canal project come to fruition none of this might have been . . . instead another of Rennie's magnificent aqueducts would have dominated the skyline here. c1920.

46 It was just downstream of Swineford Lock that the first of the navigation's three horse-ferries was sited. Although seen as an anachronism today, back in 1812 the new horse towing path was an innovation that at long last saw the end of gangs of three or four men doing the work. That said, the towing path changed sides four times between Bristol and Bath and only once with the aid of a bridge – New Bridge near Weston. The ferries were discontinued in the early 1930s when motorised barges and narrow boats were more the norm and dumb barges were towed by tugs.

Though Swineford, Saltford and Kelston Locks each had their separate lock-keeper's hut, within living memory these were manned by the one keeper. Before the war this was Harry Stiles who, when a boat arrived at Swineford, would go on ahead by bike to get Saltford ready; if he knew it was already set then he'd hop on board, bike and all, and enjoy the chat and the boat ride. Jim Crissup, skipper of the Francis & Niblett barge, the *Avon Queen*, usually left Harry a bag or two of grain (which they carried from Avonmouth to Bath) or malt (from Bath to Bristol), 'fiddling' both potential discrepancies at the Bath end (see caption 64). Perhaps it was Harry Stiles who neatly arranged the two distinctive Kennet & Avon windlasses on the lock's gate for the photographer – note too the metal extensions to the beams which, though they gave that bit of extra leverage, are remembered as being particularly inhospitable in the winter. Swineford was inhospitable in another way too, for boatmen remember it as being a real 'swine' when they were working down-river in flood conditions. In the background is Swineford Mill which, though originally part of Bristol's brass industry, ended its days as a flock mill.
c1920. *Chris Gibson Collection*

47 Known as the 'Jolly Sailor Lock', Saltford and its lockside inn have a special place in the folk memory of those who worked the river. Back in 1738 the lock was all but destroyed by 'persons unknown', presumably as a reprisal for the new navigation's success in providing the area with cheaper, though not local, coal; a painting of the lock as it was before the attack still hangs over the mantelpiece of the Jolly Sailor.

The fireplace itself bears the marks of generations of bargemen, the legacy of the custom that, whenever it was reckoned that a new recruit to the boats 'knew the Bath river', the occasion should be marked by him thrusting a red-hot poker into the fireplace's wooden surround. The oft repeated notion that he then bought a round of drinks is hotly refuted by those who recall the wages received! The inn was thus a natural meeting place for boat crews, not least because its stables housed some of the horses used on the river. It was here too during the severe floods of October 1882 that the barge *Darby*, en route from Bath with a cargo of sacked flour, broke in two and cast its cargo into the torrent. Seemingly many of the locals benefitted from the disaster by retrieving those sacks that were washed ashore.

Jim Crissup recalls similar conditions in the 1930s when he took the *Avon Queen* over Saltford weir and knocked four inches off the top; the exact measurement is known for, when the waters receded, the local paint works complained that it had lost its head of water . . . four inches of it, to be exact! The crew of the *Avon King*, Harry Niblett (Frank Niblett's son) and Jack Bevan, had a liking for mooring up overnight in the lock when they were working down from Bath – a practice that didn't please the crew of the tar barges, *Jolly* and *Darby*, who found their passage blocked the next morning!
c1925. *Tony Brown Collection*

48 The second of the Avon's three horse-ferries was just above Saltford Lock. They were large rectangular flat-bottomed craft through which a chain, fixed to each bank, was threaded; with the horse aboard, hauling on the chain would propel the boat across. Sometimes it could be tricky for the boatman, particularly working upstream when he would aim to get his barge above the line of the ferry before the horse crossed. Sometimes, too, the horse had to be blindfolded with a coat before it would board the ferry. The ferry often doubled as bathing platform for local children who would, if it were left unpadlocked, pull it out to the middle of the river; nor were they averse to deliberately leaving it on the wrong side for approaching craft. c1905. *Chris Gibson Collection*

49 Between Saltford and Kelston Locks the line of the Midland Railway crosses the river – one of five such crossings between Bitton and Green Park Station in Bath. The barge disappearing into the distance to the left of the central pier is heading downstream towards the Jolly Sailor just above which the towing path changes sides. If the barge is horse-drawn then its crew will be preparing to make use of the horse-ferry pictured above. c1910. *Tony Brown Collection*

50 Further upstream, nearer the brass mill and Kelston Lock, was the passenger ferry pictured here. The woman posing with the pole is Hannah Gregory who operated the ferry from 1886 to 1908 on behalf of her husband, Charles, who had the palsy. The alternative to the ferry was the Midland Railway bridge (photograph 49) which also boasted a walkway for pedestrians. c1900. *Tony Brown Collection*

51 This view across the top of the Saltford's Old Brass Mill takes in Kelston Lock, its attendant weir and the boathouses that have for long been a feature of this part of the river. The spot where the boat is moored above the weir is the nearest point to Saltford Tunnel on Brunel's Great Western line between Bristol and Bath, opened in August 1840. The GWR made considerable use of the river for the transport of construction materials and Brunel reported that 'At the Bristol extremity the floods have interfered with the supply of materials; and at Bath and its immediate neighbourhood the unprecedented continuation of a state of flood in the river for a long period has rendered it impossible to carry on the works . . .' That was in February, but by the summer he had forgiven the river its insubordination and is believed to have used it to carry the parts that were assembled in the sheltered workshop of Saltford Tunnel to become the engines *Fireball, Spitfire, Lynx* and *Meridian*. It is therefore likely that it was here, above Kelston weir, that Brunel himself supervised the unloading of barges or trows that unwittingly carried the seeds of their own decline. c1933.

52 During the First World War it was not unknown for the walking wounded to be treated to an outing on the river or canal (see also photograph 107). Here at Kelston Lock a passenger steamer – possibly the Bristol-based *Moss Rose* – has just such a clientele, soldiers out to make the most of their home-coming before being sent back to the trenches. As we have already seen, passenger-carrying craft made good use of the river's natural attributes and though the railway effectively put paid to such services between Bristol and Bath, the *Moss Rose* was still running such a service into the 1920s. c1917.

53 & 54 The story of the two boathouses above Kelston Lock is a tale of rivalries that span four decades. Joseph Withey built the first – the one nearest Bath – in 1896. Ten years later George Sheppard, an erstwhile landlord of the Jolly Sailor, built another almost next door. Friendly rivalry was, seemingly, not the order of the day and the friction between the two only ended in 1927 when Sheppard bought Withey's boathouse . . . though even that was done 'under the counter' for Withey did not know that Sheppard was the purchaser until after the sale. The first photograph shows how close the two were – the words 'Boat Hiring Station' are on the back of Withey's. Both boathouses were successful because their craft had access to a long lock-free part of the river which included the mile-long straight of the so-called Long Reach.

Working boatmen have cause to remember the Long Reach for several reasons. The third of the horse-ferries was at the Bath end, flanked, as was the mile-straight, by the two boisterous heads of steam of the rival GWR and Midland lines. Just before the latter's crossing, there was a series of double bends (altered slightly in the 1830s to facilitate the GWR line and straightened in 1971) lined with willow trees, the latter providing good cover, particularly at weekends, for courting couples snug in a skiff hired from Withey's or Sheppard's. Knowing this, some barge crews, having charged up the Long Reach, would cut the engine just before the bends so as not to be heard and then open them up suddenly at the first of the willows. The resulting chaos was, apparently a sight to behold: the barge would draw into itself a lot of water which would inevitably cause any skulking skiffs to experience more than a little turbulence which, combined with the sudden noise and their occupants' state of dress, had all the ingredients of a memorable afternoon on the river!

In less friendly river conditions the bends here were downright dangerous and demanded all the boatmen's skill and experience. During the '30s Henry Escott (Emmer) fell overboard from the *Avon King* here and was not missed till Kelston Lock . . . his body was recovered some time later. The skies could be unfriendly hereabouts, too, as Bill Francis found during the war; he brought the *Avon Queen* into Bath proudly displaying the scars of an encounter with a German aircraft on the mile-straight. c1920 and c1905.

55 Newton Bridge, better known today as New Bridge, is the river gateway to Bath. Here the towing path changed sides yet again, though without the inconvenience of a horse ferry. On the Kelston side there was another boating station, Cox's, which had its roots in the carrying trade. 'Old Coxy' it was who had the contract for carrying sand from the Devizes Sand Co's pits down the canal to Stothert & Pitt's riverside engineering works – the fine sand being used in the casting process. When, in 1931, this trade ceased, he set up his boating business by New Bridge. This photograph clearly shows a sharp bend leading up to the bridge, a meander that boatmen treated with the same respect as those at the end of the mile-straight; it too is no more, having been straightened out in 1971.
c1910. *Bath Reference Library*

56 Yet another boating station, this time in the shadow of Twerton Wood, took advantage of the Long Reach between Kelston and Weston Locks. Just downstream was Sparrow's crane works below which barges would sometimes tie up so that their crews could scramble up the bank to take advantage of the adjoining café (originally no more than an old railway carriage with a couple of chairs) on the Lower Bristol Road. Here Fred Short's daughter worked and, despite having a father in the carrying business, used to blush easily at the rough and ready boatmen's banter. Here too barges could top up with paraffin and petrol.
c1905. *Bath Reference Library*

57 Weston (also known as Twerton) Lock is the deepest on the river and was the last to be completed back in 1727. Nevertheless this was close enough to Bath for one enterprising Bristolian to initiate a passenger wherry service between the two cities even before the works were completed. The first lock-keeper-cum-toll-collector here was Thomas Hawkins who soon found that his £20 per annum job involved waving the heavy stick occasionally. On one occasion he refused passage to a bargeman from Bath, John Price, who concealed part of his cargo in order to avoid paying a higher toll. Hawkins' intransigence caused Price to 'brek open the gates and lock' as a result of which he was prosecuted. This was no isolated incident and in 1729 two of Simmons & Partner's bargemen who made a habit of working the same fiddle were eventually dismissed when the navigation's proprietors brought pressure to bear on the company by raising their toll from 2s per ton (1s 3d for coal) paid by others to the statutory 5s per ton.

The lock was still the centre of controversy in the 1860s when Harry Gerrish of Gerrish & Sainsbury contested GWR's illegal practice of extracting extra toll payments for using the locks at night. On September 7th, 1865 Gerrish did a John Price and broke open the gates, passed through by force and almost dared GWR to do something about it. As we shall see, this was neither the first nor the last clash between the GWR and Gerrish; on this occasion the GWR, uncharacteristically, let the matter drop. Would it be too much to speculate on whether or not the boat in question was Gerrish's barge, *Providence*?

This view of the lock was taken from Dolphin Bridge, the link between the 'mainland' and Dutch Island, though perhaps better known for its adjacent hostelry, the Dolphin Inn, which, in true waterways tradition, faces the water and not the road. Carr's cloth mill alongside the lock is no more, but the keeper's cottage on the right remains, its last 'working' inhabitants being Percy Eastup and his wife; Percy also worked as a ganger on the navigation. 1936. *Bath Reference Library*

58 During the war a bomb fell beside Dolphin Bridge and the navigation was temporarily blocked by an ample scattering of stone and rubble. The GWR were too busy to clear the obstruction so one of the carriers, Bathavon Transport, brought in a crane themselves and cleared the obstruction. The building in the background is the Dolphin Inn. 1942. *Kennet & Avon Canal Trust Collection*

59 Twerton ferry, known as the 'Royal Old Ferry', crossed the river at the Bath end of Weston Cut. This photograph of the ferry clearly shows the cut to the right and the river running down to Weston weir and Cook's mill on the left. In between is Dutch Island, so-called because of the nationality of the original brass mill owner, Nicholas Graef. The island was created by the lock cut as the connecting bridge, Dolphin, attests with its date, 1728. c1905. *Bath Reference Library*

60 This second view of the Twerton side of the 'Royal Old Ferry' includes the stern of a narrow boat; as there was no known wharf here perhaps its crew have nipped ashore to the local shop or inn. Such practices, as we have already seen, were part and parcel of the boatman's life – on one memorable occasion in 1905 the crew of a boat tried to 'fiddle' the GWR out of four hours time wasted through the poor state of navigation when in fact the time was spent in the Viaduct Inn near Dundas Wharf.
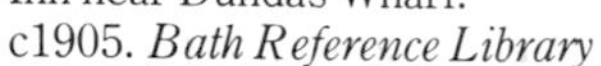
c1905. *Bath Reference Library*

61 It was Bath's gas works that saw the last commercial trade on the Kennet & Avon; the tar barges *Darby* (see photograph 18), *Jolly* and *Isabelle* made daily trips between here and Butler's at Crew's Hole until February 1967. The barges – operating as Bristol & West Tar Distillers – loaded at the wharf on the bottom right-hand of the photograph.

Gas-making began at Bath in 1814 and almost immediately took full advantage of coal from the Camerton collieries which was brought down to the river in narrow boats via the Somersetshire Coal Canal and the Kennet & Avon. Just downstream from the gas works site on the northern bank was one of the earliest 'specialist' wharves, Albion, occupied by J Smith & Co, timber merchants. In 1810 they advertised the fitting out of their Upper Bristol Road wharf with 'attendant warehouses and sufficient cranes and every other conveniency in the most substantial manner, which are now open for the accommodation of the Public for Loading, Warehousing and Shipping of all kinds of goods.' Though the company traded largely in foreign timber, they offered 'reduced prices' on any goods or freight to and from their wharf.

On the opposite bank was Fred Short's wharf which first operated as such during the late 1930s. Short was a timber merchant before he got involved with Bristol-based carriers, Francis & Niblett (later Bathavon Transport) and it was to his wharf that the *Avon King* and *Avon Queen* brought imported perishable commodities from Avonmouth destined for Bath Cold Storage in Walcot Street. This traffic began in March 1943 and included such scarcities as salmon, beans, herrings, cheese, butter, lard, dried fruit, milk, potatoes, corned beef and 'generals'. One bargeman recalls how the practice of relieving the cargo of one or two items nearly got him and his mate into trouble. Before unloading at Fred Short's, they helped themselves to six tins of corned beef, put them in a bag and stowed them in the engine hole overnight before returning to Bristol by bus. Next morning they discovered that the barge's hold had been broken into and so had to call the police. Before the police arrived, the skipper told his mate to take the bag of corned beef tins out of the engine hole and drop them over the side . . . they could always be retrieved later. After the police had come and gone the skipper told his mate to get the corned beef up. 'How?' was the nonplussed reply. 'With the boat hook, of course; just hook up the bag . . .', was the logical response. His mate's, 'Oh, but I emptied them out of the bag.' did not go down too well! c1949 *Brian Milsom Collection*

62 This view upstream takes in Victoria Suspension Bridge and, behind it, part of Stothert & Pitt's crane works. The bridge was designed by J Dredge and completed in 1836. Dredge submitted a similar design for the Clifton Suspension Bridge competition incorporating the same unusual slanted suspension rods. Stothert & Pitt (formerly Stothert & Co) had many direct connections with the river, canal and Bristol's Floating Harbour; indirectly too, it helped the stone trade by supplying the local quarries with cranes, including, in the 1850s some of the earliest steam cranes.
c1930. *Bath Reference Library*

63 The Bath and Limpley Stoke dredging and maintenance gangs pose at their steam-dredger, the *Iron Duke* below Bath's Midland Bridge – the final Midland Railway crossing into Green Park Station is in the background. Dredging of the Avon was a constant problem, particularly after GWR ownership but, although they were obliged by law to maintain the river and canal to a navigable standard, their heart was, understandably, not in it. In 1906 it was calculated that it cost the GWR about £1 to earn 10s; the financial results for the half year ending December 31st, 1905 showed that Canal Expenses came to £5,604 while income from Canal Traffic was £2,034; by 1925 the deficit had increased to £18,041.

The *Iron Duke* was one of two steam dredgers ordered from Bath's Stothert & Pitt (whose riverside works were just below the Midland Railway bridge) in 1929; the GWR's response to the considerable pressure brought to bear on them after their 1926 attempt to close the whole navigation. During the late 19th century the indefatigable Henry Gerrish had been ceaseless in his pursuit of the GWR's short-comings, particularly about the lack of dredging and shortages of water; he never saw the *Iron Duke* but no doubt his experience would have tempered any exuberance and advised against any great expectations. Within 20 years the canal was all but derelict. 1933. *Bath Reference Library*

64 Before the flood prevention scheme of the 1970s this was a familiar scene at what was Bath's New Quay, the lesser of the city's two public quays. The other, Broad Quay, saw most of the original riverside activity and only acquired the 'Broad' appendage in 1819 when the newly-opened canal spawned increased traffic and extended water-frontage; New Quay was first known as such after about 1825. On the opposite side of the river is the flour mill, known in the 1930s as the Recommissioned Mill, to which Francis & Niblett carried grain from Avonmouth in the *Avon King* and *Avon Queen*. Francis Niblett originally worked the river with the barges *Dispatch* and *Comet*; the latter was too long for the canal locks and was unsuccessfully shortened and motorised . . . in its new form it was lucky to get above one mph at full power and was soon dispensed with. Coincidentally, *Comet* began its carrying career here back in 1893 as a steam barge carrying grain and flour between Bristol and Bath for James Collins & Sons of Camden Mills, the so-called Recommissioned Mill of the '30s and '40s.

It was at the Recommissioned Mill that the crew of the *Avon Queen* 'fiddled' the missing grain that they had left for the lock-keeper at Swineford (see photograph 46). Just before the last of it was sucked out of the barge they would introduce a foreign body – usually a piece of wood – into the suction pipe; this would have the effect of throwing the valve at the top into a state of confusion which inevitably resulted in unweighed grain spilling over the floor . . . when the mess was cleared up no one could be sure how much, if any, was unaccounted for. Francis & Niblett's barges often brought malt down-river to Bristol's George's Brewery; not surprisingly the crew of the *Avon Queen* worked another 'fiddle' that was to their – and the Swineford 'keeper's – advantage. The malt was put in sacks at Weston's warehouse a few hundred yards downstream from the Recommissioned Mill, the sacks – usually about 400 – being stacked and ready for filling as and when the barge arrived. When the men doing the filling went for their tea-breaks, the ever-inventive bargemen would simply add a couple of sacks to the pile . . . and get a little something for nothing. 1937. *Bath Reference Library*

65 Although the first cargo on the new river navigation was unloaded in 1727 by Bath's Pulteney Weir, it was to the river frontage below Old Bridge that the trade inevitably graduated. While Old Bridge was a natural barrier for masted craft, the site that was to become known as Broad Quay generally gave better access to the industrial and commercial heart of the city. Before the canal opened this was a place of bustling activity: in 1805, for example, besides the warehouses of Messrs Ward, Penny, Bond and Williams (see page 11), the Quay boasted a dyer, a spectacles maker, a shoemaker, a stay-maker, a carpenter, a wheelwright, a distiller, a feltmonger, several grocers and greengrocers . . . and the Duke of York. The Quay's hinterland centred round Avon and Milk Streets, an area described in 1852 as one of '. . . filth, squalor and demoralisation, where poverty and crime lurk in miserable companionship, and where by a perversion of language, they may be said to enjoy a kind of sanctuary free from the intrusion of respectability.' It was a place for children to play and pilfer and for some, like the unfortunate 12 year old, James Longford, the fun ended in tragedy in December 1810 when he fell off a boat and drowned in the icy waters. Carriers and traders came and went but the Williams family were brewers here from the early 1780s until about 1840 while John Salmon, a carrier in his own right and agent for Bristol-based trow owners, Ames & Co, was the Avon Navigation's representative on the Quay for over 40 years from about 1800. Trows were built on the river at Bath by John Hipwood (the *Maria* in 1811 and the *Jack of Newbury* in 1814) and on the canal at Sydney Wharf (see captions 81 & 82).

By the turn of the century Broad Quay was a mere shadow of its former self; here the corn merchants clustered just as the coal merchants who were still using the canal gathered at Sydney Wharf, while those on the river took advantage of the Midland Railway's wharf opposite and just downstream of Green Park Station. Even the busiest carrier at the time, Gerrish & Co (formerly Gerrish & Sainsbury), operated from Kingston Wharf upstream of Old Bridge. This pair of narrow boats has probably come off the canal; the river level seems especially low, so low in fact that their crew has a long ladder-climb onto the quay.
c1890. *Michael Ware/Kennet & Avon Canal Trust Collection*

66 & 67 Two further images of Broad Quay show the river in more belligerent mood, its wilful waters effectively thwarting all trade. Certainly in 1894 no boat would have survived long in such conditions and probably would have sought sanctuary above Chapel Lock on the canal. It was just downstream of the left hand arch of Old Bridge that one carrier of the late 1820s, Thomas Jordan, had his own 'unofficial' wharf, described as being 'near the Old Bridge'. However temporary this may have been, it certainly had a more identifiable ring to it than an earlier base 'near the Watering troughs, upper Bristol Road, near Bath'. During the 1830s a passenger steam-boat, the *City of Bath*, left Old Bridge daily (except Sunday) for Bristol and returned the same evening. 1894 and 1937. *Bath Reference Library* and *Bath City Council*

68 Just upstream of Old Bridge was Kingston Wharf, seemingly first used as such by C & R Parker from 1830, a decade before the railway viaduct was built. In the mid-'30s the brothers, Charles and Richard, went their separate ways; both remained carriers, Richard, who had previously been Betts & Drewe's agent at Darlington Wharf, running the 'Scotch' boats on the canal and Charles working fly boats from Kingston Wharf. By 1849 Charles' boats are carrying to Hungerford, Newbury and Reading three times a week but by the early 1850s he has joined the rush to the railways and his erstwhile agent at Devizes, Daniel Phipp, has taken over the wharfside business. In 1864 Phipp sold out to Gerrish & Sainsbury, the driving force of which, as we have already seen, was Henry Gerrish.

Gerrish's brushes with the GWR were as frequent as they were often farcical. If there weren't disputes about the state of the navigation there were disagreements about toll charges. In May 1866 Gerrish claimed to have been overcharged 2s 8d by the practice of calculating tolls to the nearest penny *above* any fraction of a penny; fuel was added to the fire when he further claimed that Old Bridge to Hanham Mills was one mile less than in the toll tables. The GWR compromised but still reckoned that Gerrish & Sainsbury owed them £1,385 in unpaid tolls and duly sued them. Not for the last time did the GWR lose their battle with Gerrish; they subsequently had to pay compensation of £660 and most of the costs of a long-drawn-out court case. Little wonder he called two of his boats *Faith* and *Prudence*!

The 'Sainsbury' half of the partnership dropped out in 1873 around the time that the company first started using steamers on the river. Such craft could only work the canal by arrangement with GWR and as Gerrish was hardly their favourite person it could explain the family connection with the Devizes-based Bath & Bristol Steam Boat Co (see photograph 78). One of their most regular customers was Bath's J B Bowler who also supplied them with parts for the steamers.

Another dispute arose with the GWR in 1893 over their planned reduction in railway carriage rates; Gerrish wrote to all his customers thus:

> 'As we understand the Railway Companies are considerably reducing their recently advanced Rates for Carriage, we beg respectfully to inform you, that, although the notice we received from the Railway Company who own the Waterway, of a great increase in Toll charges, has been withdrawn, and the question is still before the Board of Trade, we shall reduce our charges from the present date.
> Thanking you for your support in the past, and hoping for a continuance of the same.'

The matter was settled by the Canal Tolls and Charges Order Confirmation Act of 1894 whereby tolls on the Kennet & Avon were reduced to about ½d per ton per mile.

In 1904 Giddings & Willis (both had worked for Gerrish and the former was also involved with the Bath & Bristol Steam Boat Co) took over the business but based themselves first at Broad Quay and then across the river from the wharf of maltsters, J D Taylor & Son. Two years later the partnership became White & Willis and continued operating as such on the river until 1912.
c1905. *Maurice Scott Collection*

69 The narrow boat pictured here is, like the crowds lining both river banks, a helpless onlooker to the aftermath of the Widcombe Bridge disaster. On Wednesday June 6th, 1877 a throng of day trippers heading for the Bath & West Show atop Beechen Cliff packed the length of the 'Halfpenny' river footbridge behind the station waiting to pay their toll when it collapsed. The *Bath Chronicle* graphically described the scene:

> 'At eleven O'clock the flooring of the bridge was seen to bend, a crash followed, the tie-rods and girders became separated from the masonry and the holiday crowd previously standing on the bridge were suddenly shot, as it were, down two inclined planes into the centre of the river Avon. Others fell on the towpath, and others were buried beneath the falling debris. Considering the appalling nature of the accident, the number of deaths (some nine or ten persons) was less than might have been expected.'

Widcombe, the hamlet in the background, extended across the entrance to the canal which is just off the picture to the left. Much of these terraces have now gone due to the road improvement schemes of the 1970s. 1877. *Bath Reference Library*

70 This view of the Dolemeads (the cluster of houses between the entrance to the canal and the second GWR viaduct) illustrates how it acquired its nickname of 'Mud Island'. The entrance to the canal is somewhere under the deluge on the extreme right in the shadow of Thimble Mill's chimney. During the floods of 1809 a child in its cradle was carried off from a cottage here by the swollen waters of the river but was snatched up from the torrent by some bargemen at Old Bridge and returned to its parents.

Such conditions gave heart to the advocates of a Bath & Bristol Canal to circumvent the river and in 1811 a Parliamentary enquiry took evidence from various traders used to its vicissitudes. John Smith of Albion Wharf (see caption 61) maintained that it could take anything from one to ten days to navigate between Bristol and Bath depending on the river's conditions – on one occasion he had to pay *ten* men 8s each to haul his barge against the flood. Another hazard was the tendency for millers to let off water when the river was low – as a result of which one of Smith's barges was sunk and £75 worth of damage done. In his evidence John Salmon, the agent to the river's proprietors, produced some startling statistics: loaded to 40 tons, a barge would average only 28 to 30 voyages between Bristol and Bath per year; at the time there were only 16 barges using the river regularly and there was once a 14-day period without a single barge trading at the Quay. 1894. *Bath Reference Library*

71 Ignoring the entrance to the canal for the moment, we follow the river round to its limit of navigation, Pulteney Weir. The derelict and decaying building on the right marks the northerly entrance to the canal and was probably originally an extremity of Ralph Allen's wharf at the Dolemeads (see also page 13). As one of the proprietors of the Avon Navigation, Ralph Allen was quick to use the river to carry the local freestone downstream to Bristol and beyond. In 1726 he bought the quarries at Combe Down above Bath; demand was such that within five years he had established an ingenious tramroad down the hillside to his wharf thus reducing the price from 10s per ton to 7s 6d. From here up to 1,800 tons a year was loaded onto barges bound for Bristol and what wasn't used in building works here was shipped to Belfast and Dublin. After Allen's death in 1764 the tramroad was dismantled. Stone continued to be carried by river and, of course, eventually by canal but via Bath's other wharves and quays. During the late 1860s and early 1870s William Large built barges on the river here while brother James was doing the same on the canal at Darlington Wharf. From 1899 Frederick Charles Cox was also building boats at Dolemeads, the same Cox who carried sand from Devizes to Stothert & Pitt at Bath and later ran the boating station at New Bridge.

Just beyond the second railway crossing there was another small wharf backing onto Railway Place where, between 1913 and 1921, Sydney Hawkins operated a small cargo service with *Argo, Jane* and *Jenny*. Here too Messrs J T Holmes had their timber yard until the beginning of the war when they moved to Bristol from where, in 1941, their barge, *Comet* (previously owned by Francis & Niblett) tried to take a cargo of timber up the canal to Claverton on behalf of the Ministry of Supply. Though *Comet* was only loaded to a draught of 3ft, it soon experienced difficulties on the by now shallow and badly maintained canal and the trip was abandoned; *Comet* itself, as we have seen (caption 64), could scarcely have helped matters.
c1859. *Bath Reference Library*

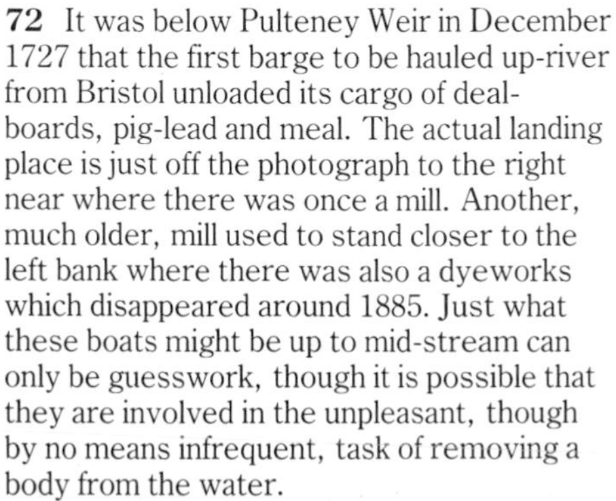

72 It was below Pulteney Weir in December 1727 that the first barge to be hauled up-river from Bristol unloaded its cargo of deal-boards, pig-lead and meal. The actual landing place is just off the photograph to the right near where there was once a mill. Another, much older, mill used to stand closer to the left bank where there was also a dyeworks which disappeared around 1885. Just what these boats might be up to mid-stream can only be guesswork, though it is possible that they are involved in the unpleasant, though by no means infrequent, task of removing a body from the water.
c1925. *Bath Reference Library*

73 The completion of the Widcombe Locks in November 1810, though acknowledged in the local press, did not generate popular excitement. The waiting had been too long, work began on the flight around the turn of the century but was then abandoned and replaced by an adjacent tramroad while energies were concentrated elsewhere. When the works were completed, the locks proved to be a problem in that lockful after lockful of precious water naturally tumbled down into the Avon.

By 1813 the water supply had been augmented by Claverton Pumping Station (see caption 94) but in times of shortage and drought the locks had to be closed. In the early 1830s the Canal Company acquired Thimble Mill (to the left of Lower Lock) and installed a pump to lift water from the Avon up to the basin above Abbey View Lock from where it was pumped to the 9-mile pound above Top Lock. Early maps of the canal indicate that Abbey View Lock was originally called 'Rasamar', a name that at first glance has no obvious local connections. One theory is that it might be one of several known variations of 'Reskemar', a common name within the Allen family. Ralph Allen was long dead before the canal was built but he did have close associations with the Avon Navigation and locally at least his name is remembered with an affection verging on reverence. c1920. *Kennet & Avon Canal Trust Collection*

74 Water shortages continued even into the Railway Age when traffic was greatly reduced. During the summer months it was usual for narrow boats to be restricted to using the locks in pairs to save water but, needless to say, one local carrier was all but a law unto himself . . . Henry Gerrish! In September 1865 he defied the restriction and broke open the padlocked gates of Lower Lock and worked up the flight . . . conceivably in his fly boat, *Antagonist.* As Gerrish probably knew, the GWR was powerless to enforce such constraints on carriers and the only action taken was to point out that the rule was there to the benefit of all traders. The large ponds between locks – such as the one here that goes off to the left behind Thimble Mill – were in effect mini-reservoirs where water could be stored to reduce the frequency of shortages.
c1907. *Maurice Scott Collection*

75 A pair of narrow boats – in accordance with GWR restrictions – works up the Widcombe flight between Lower and Chapel Locks, the latter so-named from the adjacent Baptist Chapel with its roof-top message. In the mid 1860s two waterside inns sprang up along the canal here: one, the Boatman's Arms, was at the end of the terrace, Waterloo Buildings, to the right of the locks; the second, the Canal Tavern, was by Bridge Lock.
c1910. *Maurice Scott Collection*

76 At the extremity of the side pond above Bridge Lock was Widcombe Wharf. Around 1810 the site was occupied by a boat and barge builder, S Bird, but for 30 years from the 1830s it was the base of Mary Merry, a wood and coal merchant who, unlike most of her competitors, made no additional claims to fame such as being a wharfinger or bargemaster. From 1864 George Stockden was the incumbent here dealing largely, like his predecessor, in coal from the Somerset collieries brought in by canal. Stockden gave way to his erstwhile partner, George Morgan, who was the last trader here to use the canal in 1917.
c1905. *Chris Gibson Collection*

77 An idyllic setting at Wash House Lock, the swans a bonus to the patient photographer. The iron footbridge at the tail of the chamber was, like that at Top Lock, cast at the Stothert foundry some time after 1815. Robert Kilvert (1803–1882), a relative of George Stothert, was brought up in the adjacent Caroline Buildings and recalled how he and his childhood peers used to slip on the woodwork of the lock gates when they wanted to cross the chamber and how 'one poor fellow named Henry Scarfe' was found to be 'quite dead from falling in the lock and drowning'. Thus both bridges were probably a later addition, a theory given further credence by the fact that they are clearly built atop the chamber rather than a part of it. Stothert also supplied – but did not make – the two iron bridges, ERECTED ANNO 1800, in Sydney Gardens; these originated at the Coalbrookdale works in Shropshire and were probably brought down the Severn to Bristol by trow. c1910. *Maurice Scott Collection*

78 A pair of narrow boats belonging to the Devizes-based Bath & Bristol Steam Boat Co is about to begin their descent of the Widcombe locks. Before the turn of the century steamers were still relatively rare on the navigation and carriers intending to use such craft on the canal had to have GWR's permission. The Bath & Bristol Steam Boat Co began carrying in the 1880s under the direction of Gerrish & Co's Devizes agent, James Giddings.

Gerrish, in order to work steamers on the canal, may have set up this separate company to circumvent the need to crawl to the GWR and/or mend his ways. Whatever the truth of the matter, this new company soon ceased trading though not without one notable brush with the GWR . . . involving another Gerrish, Harry. It was the custom to close the Bath locks each Whitsuntide in order to clear the backlog of maintenance on the 9-mile pound between Bradford-on-Avon and Bath but in May 1889 the padlocked gates were no deterrent to Gerrish who simply forced his way through. This time he was properly sued for wilful damage and fined.

The wharf to the left of the loaded boat was, until the end of the century, the Somersetshire Coal Canal Company's Bath base, the SCCC having vacated Sydney Wharf in 1810 when the Kennet & Avon opened. At right angles to the wharf is the company's stabling block and opposite, on the towpath side, the lock-keeper's cottage and what appears to be a horse.

c1890. *Philip Wilson/Kennet & Avon Canal Trust Collection*

79 Alongside the redundant wharf and crane of the maltsters, Bairds, just up from Top Lock, was the last resting place for the 'Scotch' boats that, in the 1830s, were the canal's star attraction. They were originally run between Bath and Bradford-on-Avon by Richard Parker; his 1837 advertisement, reproduced below, speaks for itself.

R. PARKER'S
CELEBRATED AND SWIFT SAILING
SCOTCH BOAT
Leaves BRADFORD at 8 in the Morning, and 4 in the Afternoon;
And BATH at 11 in the Morning, and 6 in the Evening;
From 1st April to the end of September.
And from BRADFORD, at 9 in the Morning, and 3 in the Afternoon;
And BATH, at 11 in the Morning, and 5 in the Evening;
From 1st October to the end of March:
(SUNDAYS EXCEPTED).
☞ *COACHES convey Passengers from* BATH *to* BRISTOL, *and an OMNIBUS from* BRADFORD *to* TROWBRIDGE, *on arrival of the Boat.*

Parker's business was taken over by Packer & Kiver around 1840 and a new element to the 'swift sailing Scotch Boat' service was added. Richard Packer lived in the Claverton Hotel (formerly Richard Parker's home and known as Combe Villa), a large house overlooking Dundas Wharf to which a newer and shorter version of the boats ran daily (see page 15). An unsubstantiated local story associates this same house with bawdy goings on to which a wealthy clientele were brought along the canal by boat. The Packer & Kiver boat would seem to be the obvious link in the chain, possibly an extra-curricular service put on after the public one returned to Bath at 7pm.

Both this and the regular Bradford-on-Avon service operated from 'the back of Sydney Gardens', just east of the second tunnel. The boats in the photograph are almost certainly Packer & Kiver's redundant fleet, the service having ended sometime in the early 1850s when competition from the railways – and a GWR-imposed speed restriction – proved too much. Further towards Top Lock a trow is tied up alongside the stabling block next to the Somersetshire Coal Canal Wharf, rare proof that such vessels did indeed trade on the canal. It is likely that the trow here is the *Matchless*, the last of several to be built by Francis Hooper between 1839 and 1855 at Sydney Wharf (see captions 81 & 82). c1856. *Tim Wheeldon Collection*

80 Bathwick Bridge was the gateway to one of the busiest parts of the canal, Sydney Wharf. The short length between here and the first of the tunnel bridges (see photograph 84) began its active life well before the canal was finally completed in 1810 . . . when this photograph was taken all that fervour and expectancy was scarcely even a memory. Here the beneficiaries of a dying artery are inspecting their inheritance, seeking confirmation, if such were necessary, that the Kennet & Avon had passed away. Fortunately, before the final nail was resolutely driven home, the body began to stir. 1956. *Bath Reference Library*

81 & 82 Two boat-less views of Sydney Wharf that barely do justice to this bustling heart of the canal at Bath. But it was not always so for, before the Widcombe locks opened in 1810, the wharf was the domain of the Somersetshire Coal Canal Company and their agents R Carpenter & Son and few of the inhabitants of the surrounding cluster of freestone cottages had any obvious connection with the canal. When the SCCC vacated the wharf the Carpenters continued to deal in coal from the Timsbury and Camerton collieries while John Peacock dealt in timber. John Andras who at the time ran a packet boat from Bath also lived nearby.

Slowly, almost imperceptibly, the wharf gathered to itself people keen to exploit, in one way or another, this new artery. Peacock was soon a bargemaster, a wharfinger and a general carrier; Thomas Peacock took over the reins in 1826, added coal merchant and corn & flour factor to the repertoire, and by the 1840s his wife, Mary, was in charge of a carrying business that claimed its own wharf along Bristol's Temple Back. Similarly, from the late 1840s the Hooper and Hawkins families had long associations with the wharf, both as carriers and landlords of one of the wharfside alehouses, the Bargeman's Tavern. Francis Hooper began in the early 1830s as landlord of the Cleveland Arms; he started up the Bargeman's Tavern around 1845 (for a time, in 1855, the community supported a third alehouse, the Alma Tavern) and was also involved in carrying and boat-building – he is known to have built five trows, the *Derby, Trial,* two *Hannahs* and the *Matchless,* the barge *Newport* and probably the trows, *Fanny* and *Ann* as well. His son, another Francis, ended his days on the wharf in 1873 as a wharfinger and bargemaster, having also been landlord of the Bargeman's Tavern in 1860.

Eli Cornelius Hawkins first came to Sydney Wharf in 1847 as a carrier and beer retailer but, after a brief stint at the Bargeman's Tavern, vacated the wharf for six years, returning in 1858 as a wharfinger. Three years on, Eli Cornelius was no more but the Hawkins tradition was picked up in 1868 by Thomas who quickly worked his way up the ranks: wharfinger's assistant (at Darlington Wharf), wharfinger's foreman (at the SCC wharf) and finally, from 1874, coal merchant and carrier at Sydney Wharf. In 1891 Hawkins' fleet of narrow boats, *Blanche, Bessie, Rosetta, Emma, Alice,* and *Jenny* became the basis of the Bath & Bristol Steam Boat Co's fleet; some of these, presumably, had steam engines fitted. It is likely that the Sydney Hawkins that operated on the river after 1913 (see caption 71) was part of the same family . . . conceivably even that he was so-called after the wharf.

The two old hands, Euclid Shaw and Aurelius Drewe, witnessed most of these changes, either from here or from Darlington Wharf. But it was Aurelius who, from his new position as the K&ACC's Traffic Manager after June 1848, oversaw the demise of a short-lived way of life. Drewe tried to interest the Canal Company in investing in the Severn trade and a fleet of trows – he even purchased one without their permission and was duly reprimanded. In 1850 he resigned his position in the hope that he could take the trade over on his own account and prove his point; his offer was refused and, perhaps almost as an act of defiance, he joined the GWR as a goods superintendent!

Thus after 1852 trade to and from the wharf inevitably declined. Though some general carrying continued, it became little more than a coal wharf with several coal merchants, such as Joseph Lansdown, Job Nash, Henry Cox and George Dike (these last two having moved from Darlington Wharf), operating from there. In the 1880s Dike had his own small fleet of narrow boats, *Magdala, Rose* and *St George,* though the latter sank at the wharf. By the early part of the new century Dike's erstwhile partner, G Seers, and Thomas Hawkins are the only traders left using the canal regularly; by 1911 Hawkins, the sole survivor, had moved on.
c1939 and 1956. *Bath Reference Library*

83 John Vaughan came to Sydney Wharf about 1830 from Hampton Row, itself a canal-side location opposite Darlington Wharf before the diversion of the canal here in 1839 to facilitate the railway. Being a quarrymaster too, Vaughan probably had close connections with the canal and its carriers and may well have built some of the outbuildings and houses that supported this flourishing community. Likewise other tradesmen on the wharf such as Charles Cannon, a farrier (William Cannon was also a farrier on Broad Quay), John Jennings, a wheelwright, and W Robinson, a brewer, would have gained much from the canal. Others, like the coal and corn merchants, had more obvious connections with the waterway's trade. Some, like coal merchant J Clarke, progressed into carrying; during the 1820s Clarke, Robins & Co operated daily fly boats from the wharf but about 1830 sold out to S & J Provis – remaining as their Honey Street agents. On the other hand another coal merchant, Joseph Landsdown, went about his wharf-side trade for 30 years from 1832.

John Vaughan retired in 1857, though his once-busy cart remained on the wharf almost as a rustic memorial to what had been. c1859. *Bath Reference Library*

84 At the eastern extremity of Sydney Wharf (sometimes known as Pinches Wharf) the canal plunged under the K&ACC's headquarters from the 1820s, Cleveland House, and into the sylvan splendour of Sydney Gardens. The Gardens predated the canal and, it being a popular diversion for the genteel citizens of Bath, the Canal Company had to indulge in some delicate negotiations to route the canal this way. 2,000 guineas was the 'compromise' agreed in 1798. In 1864, 12 years after GWR ownership, Cleveland House was vacated and the canal's affairs moved to Paddington. Between the cellars of Cleveland House and the roof of the tunnel-bridge pictured here there is a narrow shaft that has given rise to the oft-repeated theory that verbal messages and/or packages were once passed through to passing boatmen. The practicalities of such a system must throw doubt on its accuracy. As the bridge in front of Cleveland House is a turnover bridge (where the towing path changed sides without the need to unhitch the horse), barges and narrow boats might well pass under the 10in × 8in orifice at a leisurely pace . . . but what would be the point of such a hit-and-miss communication shaft when the Canal Company had such close connections with carriers at the two nearest wharves, Sydney and Darlington, where any important messages could be sure of getting through? That said, the purpose of the shaft remains a mystery. c1895. *Bath Reference Library*

85 A photograph frustrating for what it doesn't show! On the extreme right there is the merest glimpse of the eastern end of Sydney Gardens, on the towpath side of which passengers once boarded the 'Scotch' boats for their excursion to the Claverton Hotel or trip to Bradford-on-Avon. Just inside the tunnel-bridge, rings on either side were supposedly linked on Sundays by a GWR-imposed chain in order to protect the good and God-fearing citizens of Bath from the noisy boats and their crew. There is no record of the same arrangement on the adjacent railway line, nor of Henry Gerrish's acquiescence!

On the extreme left is the beginning of what was Darlington Wharf . . . and in between the skeletal remains of a narrow boat perhaps even the very one so dramatically caught by the camera in the previous photograph. Darlington Wharf not only ended its days with the appendage 'Old', but was also the last 'working' outpost in Bath of the GWR-run canal during the 1860s. The wharf was Betts & Drewe's base after they vacated Broad Quay in 1825 until the early 1840s by which time they shared it with the boat-builder, William Hooper. By 1846 it had already acquired the 'Old' tag, and Euclid Shaw and his sons, James and Thomas, were Hooper's temporary neighbours until the latter became landlord of the Crown at nearby Bathwick. Aurelius Drewe, as we have seen, went down to Sydney Wharf to run the K&ACC's new fleet; when that failed and the canal had passed into GWR ownership the carrying that remained became concentrated at Sydney Wharf leaving Old Darlington as little more than a token base. Even the GWR's agent here, William Hull, was running his own small carrying business from Sydney Wharf in the 1860s. At the same time James Large brought boat-building back to the wharf and William Horsell and others were trading in coal from the Somerset collieries.

During the late 1860s the wharf embarked upon a new and totally unexpected era. In 1867 a committee of the Bath Local Board of Health looked at three canal sites for the provision of a public bathing place. Those at the back of Caroline Buildings (between Wash House and Rasamar Locks) and at the basin by Thimble Mill were rejected, as was that of a 'pontoon barge of corrugated iron', in favour of Old Darlington Wharf. From 1860 the wharf had been leased by coal merchant William Horsell (who also ran the nearby Crown) and while negotiations continued between the committee and GWR during 1868, Horsell tried to interest them in leasing the whole wharf. In this he was unsuccessful and the bathing place was established in 1869 all but rubbing shoulders with boat building and coal yards. Coal merchant George Dike was the last to operate from the wharf; he moved down to Sydney Wharf in 1877.
1956. *Bath Reference Library*

86 Folly Swing Bridge is just east of Darlington Wharf; for boats working up from the river it was the first of many swing bridges to be negotiated. The inventiveness of John Rennie, the canal's architect, ensured that such bridges on the Kennet & Avon swung with less effort than elsewhere . . . thanks, that is, to the ball-bearing. Under the swing-bridge are two sets of stop gates, one pair of which would have been forced closed by the surge of water that would result from a sudden breach. As we shall see (captions 101 and 102), the 9-mile pound was prone to such calamities and the 18 sets of such gates in 7½ miles illustrate the seriousness of the problem.

Down towards the railway (on the left) there used to be an alehouse, the Folly Tavern. In 1862 Thomas Osmond took over the site to run, for 25 years, the Victorian equivalent of an amusement park. The Cremorne Pleasure Gardens were open each Monday and Wednesday evening throughout the summer and offered the bright young sparks of Bath a range of up-market wines, spirits and beers, foreign cigars, music and dancing, the longest and most comfortable bowling saloon in Bath, quoits, Aunt Sally, Madame Claudet, gymnasiums and a variety of other outdoor amusements . . . all of which were brilliantly illuminated at dusk. It was clearly not the passing boatman's scene, nevertheless the canal must have reverberated to the fun and frolics of this eccentric side of Bath's night life. Sadly there is no record of Henry Gerrish ever having crossed swords with Thomas Osmond or his clientele!

In 1887 Cremorne passed into the hands of the GWR after which only the tavern, known as the Grosvenor Brewery, remained. It is the sign for this, advertising wines and spirits and home-brewed ale, that stands by the bridge . . . though it was best remembered by boatmen for its 'faggots and beer'. c1907. *Chris Gibson Collection*

87 During the early part of the 20th century Robbins, Lane & Pinnegar of Honey Street took over the 'watchdog' mantle from Henry Gerrish and were as relentless in their pursuit, as they saw it, of the shortcomings of the GWR. In 1905 they had been given an undertaking that the canal would not be allowed to deteriorate further. In 1929 a yardstick was established in the shape of their barge *Unity* which, laden to a draught of around 3ft 6in, should have been able to pass through the canal. A dredging programme followed in the early 1930s and worked its way east from Bath using the new steam dredgers built by Stothert & Pitt (see also photograph 63). Every year Colonel Lane of Robbins, Lane & Pinnegar made a point of bringing *Unity* to and from Bristol though on one occasion his trip was disputed by GWR and Hubert Ashmead of F A Ashmead & Sons had to verify in court that he had seen *Unity* in Bristol. The dredger photographed here is between Folly and Candy's Bridges near Bathampton. c1930. *Kennet & Avon Canal Trust Collection*

88 & 89 The larger photograph was taken from alongside the stone bridge, Candy's, featured in the second, smaller, picture. A Victorian gent sitting on a fallen tree is scarcely worth recording except that the same photographer not only took both these photographs but also number 77, the 'Scotch' boats at Top Lock. Is it beyond the bounds of possibility that the pipe-smoking gentleman has some sort of connection with the canal, a gentleman closely associated with its owners, GWR . . . Brunel? Or is it no more than an 'I-was-there-when-this-tree-was-struck-by-lightning' photograph? c1856.

90 Lockless waters such as the 9-mile pound between Bradford-on-Avon and Bath lent themselves to passenger trip-boats like the one photographed here heading east near Candy's Bridge. The chances of its passengers espying a working boat were quite slim; in 1906 it was observed that 'the actual traffic on the Kennet and Avon at the western end would not exceed more than about three or four boats a day . . .' The sender of this picture-postcard certainly had a good time and recorded the occasion simply: 'It was lovely, we went over the aqueduct.' The fact that she was able to send her friend a card of the actual trip-boat shows a certain amount of organisation on the part of its operator.
c1920. *Michael Ware/Kennet & Avon Canal Trust Collection*

91 William Harbutt, the inventor of plasticine, moved into his new canalside premises at Bathampton in 1900. The former flour mill was a five-storey building with a 'cat head' projecting from the fourth floor and over the canal. Harbutt's used the waterway for the delivery of coke for their small gas engine and, as can be seen here, empty barrels were taken away by narrow boat. Today the narrow boat is fairly well-defined in terms of its 'narrowness' – usually around 6ft 10ins. In the canal's heyday it was more of a hit-and-miss affair; 'narrow' boats could be anything from 6ft 1in to 6ft 10in and so-called 'wide' boats or barges normally between 10ft and 14ft, sometimes even wider.
1905. *Kennet & Avon Canal Trust Collection*

92 Harbutt's Mill and the George Inn dominated the canal at Bathampton but both predate it; parts of the inn are believed to go back to the 14th century. Neither would have been by the canal at all had Rennie's original plans come to fruition for the route into Bath was to be via a 5-lock flight from Bathampton to Batheaston Weir on the Avon and a lock by Pulteney Weir. This was abandoned in order to ensure all-the-year-round navigation to Bath, an extended river section would only have made the city inaccessible at times of flood. c1890. *Bath Reference Library*

93 The weather did not affect only the river. Not infrequently the canal suffered from lack of water, sometimes due to inadequate supply, wastage or drought. Similarly the winter months could bring stoppages caused by ice, particularly so here at Bathampton where the channel narrows to swing round between the George and Harbutt's Mill (see photograph 92). For boatmen, lost time was lost money; for the locals it was a chance to brush up on their skating technique: it was not unknown for the lunch-break at Harbutt's to be extended to allow the workers to take advantage of this new amenity on their doorstep.

Round a series of double bends from Bathampton Bridge was Hampton Quarry Wharf, the canal terminus of the tramroad down from quarries on Bathampton Down. In 1798, in order to appease the canal's shareholders (who had every reason to expect soon to be in a position to exploit trade on the Somersetshire Coal Canal), the Canal Committee accelerated work on the Claverton to Bath section. Advertisements were placed in the local press inviting barge builders to '. . . contract for building and finding all materials for six barges in the parish of Bath Hampton on the banks of the Kennet and Avon Canal . . .' The SCC traffic didn't materialise but no doubt these barges soon found themselves carrying stone from the Canal Company's own quarries at Conkwell near Dundas Aqueduct (see caption 98). But it was the inferior quality of this and a second quarry at Winsley (see caption 104) that necessitated the use of the stone from Bathampton as envisaged in the following advertisement in 1808:

'Inclined Plane. Any Person or Persons willing to contract for forming, making and completing an Inclined Plane Road from Bathampton Quarries to the Kennet and Avon Canal, a distance of about 800 yards are desired to send their proposals (sealed up) to Mr Bennett, engineer, St James's Parade, Bath – Plans, Sections and specifications may be seen at Mr Bennett's Office.'

1905. *Bath Reference Library*

94 A horse-drawn narrow boat negotiates one of the bends between Bathampton and Claverton, where water was lifted from the river below via Claverton Pumping Station. Originally a grist mill belonging to the Duke of Somerset, it was not acquired by the Canal Company until 1810; work on rebuilding and installation of the machinery began in 1813. In the meantime water levels were maintained by several small natural feeders, the water coming down through Bradford Lock and off the Somersetshire Coal Canal . . . all of which was totally inadequate in the summer months. All these boatmen would have seen was the outlet pipe protruding from the canal bank, the waters of the Avon, theoretically at least, gushing forth day and night.

In 1833 Brunel inspected the river valley around Claverton and was clearly not impressed:

> 'The side of the hill is a rotten description oolite laying on clay. Many slips have occurred owing no doubt to the washing of the clay by the river and considerably assisted by the bad management of the canal. Blackwell the Canal engineer, a bigotted, obstinate *practical man* says the road [the railway] will make the hill slip, but could not tell us why.'

It was not only at Claverton that the canal was perched precariously on the valley wall; even before the Railway Age much of the 9-mile pound was prone to landslips and blow outs though the Limpley Stoke to Bradford-on-Avon section suffered most.
c1915. *Michael Ware/Kennet & Avon Canal Trust Collection*

95 Bath-bound, one of the Midland Railway's three horse-drawn narrow boats, *No 3,* negotiates Dundas Bridge where the towing path changed sides. William Hooper, who previously worked the *Bessie* for Thomas Hawkins of Sydney Wharf, was the master and possibly had family connections with Francis Hooper, a carrier from the wharf in the 1850s and '60s (see captions 81 & 82). It is ironic that the Midland Railway should find itself operating from Bradford-on-Avon on a canal owned by one of its railway rivals, the GWR. *No 3* has clearly acquired a human cargo as well as whatever lies under the sheets. This practice may well have started on a casual basis but, as indicated by photograph 108, it does seem to have become a feature of the Midland's service between Bath and Bradford-on-Avon.

The Midland's three narrow boats were acquired in 1891 probably to replace rather than augment the existing barge fleet which had been operating from around 1884. The trade was such that barges were simply unnecessary nor was it long before the narrow boats were themselves redundant; by 1911 both *No 1* and *No 3* had moved on to Robbins, Lane & Pinnegar of Honey Street to be renamed *Jane* and *Kate* respectively. c1900. *Kennet & Avon Canal Trust Collection*

96 Viewed from in front of Dundas Bridge, this panorama takes in Dundas Wharf and crane, the entrance to the Somersetshire Coal Canal and the left-hand sweep of the canal towards Dundas Aqueduct. The two small stone tablets in the foreground supported a roller around which a chain, connected to a plug in the canal bed, could be wound. Through this simple mechanism the canal could be drained for re-puddling and maintenance, a common requirement on the 9-mile pound. The second cow from the left hides almost all of a tall cast-iron corner-post which stopped the towing rope from 'cutting the corner' and disappearing into the trees and shrubs. On the wharf opposite is a small toll-house (out of view), a warehouse and a crane. In 1884 the Midland Railway's barge *Jenny* fractured the crane's chain and the company was fined £14 14s 7d. Smoke rises from the lock-keeper's cottage on the Somersetshire Coal Canal; between the cottage and the towpath bridge are what seem to be the high-and-dry remains of one of the shorter 'Scotch' boats.

The entrance lock to the Somersetshire Coal Canal had a rise and fall of only seven inches and could accommodate only narrow beamed craft. But it was not always so for, as recent excavation of the chamber has shown, it was once a wide lock which gave the Kennet & Avon's barges access to the basin beyond. Exactly what circumstances or rivalries led to the narrowing of the lock remain a mystery. What is certain is that from the 1820s Dundas Wharf was the main gauging station for traffic leaving the SCC, as evidenced by the gauging blocks – large slabs with which a boat's displacement could be calculated – that can be seen on the wharfside.

Traffic on the SCC ceased in 1898 and the canal was abandoned six years later. One of the last traders was Adam Wragg of Seend in Wiltshire whose boats, *Mary, Queen* and *Phoebe* carried coal from Dunkerton Colliery; *Phoebe* and captain, Dan Harris, have the distinction, if distinction it be, to have been the last to work through the SCC's stop-lock and re-join the Kennet & Avon here at Dundas. c1900. *D M McDougall/Kennet & Avon Canal Trust Collection*

97 Dundas Wharf in festive mood as an outing from Trowbridge (see also photograph 109) takes advantage of the fine weather. With the closure of the SCC the crane is all but redundant, the gauging blocks a convenient seat for the children. Whatever the occasion, the outing was enlivened by the musical trio standing on the bows . . . aided and abetted by a curious youngster. Such outings had always been a feature of the canal for John Rennie and his colleagues had cut a broad swathe through some of the most glorious countryside in the south of England. None more so than the Limpley Stoke valley with its sylvan delights cascading down to the water and the river Avon an ever-sparkling companion. The undecorated wharf-side boat is seemingly not part of the festivities and appears to be securely chained to one of the gauging blocks.
c1905. *Tim Wheeldon Collection*

98 The spectacular splendour of Dundas Aqueduct is scarcely done justice by this photograph taken from the A36 above. In the centre foreground the arm of the wharfside crane points towards the roof of the warehouse and Bath while behind the trees on the right is the redundant entrance to the SCC. Across the aqueduct, on the corner just as the canal swings round to the right, is the site of the erstwhile terminus of the tramroad down the hillside from Conkwell quarry. The quarry was opened by the Canal Company in 1801 in the hope that it could supply better quality stone than that available at the time for the works on the canal. Such hopes were not fulfilled and two years later another quarry was opened at Murhill near Winsley (see caption 104). The canalside buildings on the right comprised a lengthsman's cottage and a stable-block for horses used for towing. In the late 1850s the roar of steam first intruded upon this peaceful valley.
c1915. *D L McDougall/Kennet & Avon Canal Trust Collection*

99 A weed-choked basin, the bridge over the entrance to the SCC gone, a derelict toll-office, a redundant crane and an abandoned barge were the inevitable result of inactivity and the virtual surrender of the Kennet & Avon to the ravages of time.
1956. *Bath Reference Library*

100 An empty Bristol-registered Honey Street barge approaches Limpley Stoke Bridge heading towards Bath. It may be that the barge is being delivered by Robbins, Lane & Pinnegar (formerly Robbins & Co) to become part of United Alkali's 'precious stone' fleet (see photograph 15). Back in 1811 the local Parson, Mr Valentine, indulged in a little canalside trade when he tried to sell . . . a quantity of Elm and Ash at Limpley Stoke by the canal. c1892. *Kennet & Avon Canal Trust Collection*

101 & 102 The stretch of canal between Limpley Stoke and Bradford-on-Avon was the most notorious length in terms of its susceptibility to leaks, landslips and blow-outs. Under GWR ownership what maintenance there was tended to be concentrated in the week-long Whitsuntide stoppage for re-puddling. This particular stretch of the canal passes over deep-fissured limestone and it was the underground movement of water associated with this that caused the problems. On one such occasion in 1902 a maintenance boat was carried off to the Avon below through a 30ft breach in the bank . . . luckily the maintenance gang had just stepped ashore. It was for just such eventualities that the stop-gates here and elsewhere were installed; in theory, as soon as the first surge of water was sensed, these should have snapped shut and held in the water either side of the breach. These photographs, looking towards the same set of stop-gates from opposite sides, were taken during the annual stoppage. c1910. *British Rail*

103 It was not all breaches and maintenance. People even got pleasure from the canal and its environs as is clearly illustrated here at the same stop-gate narrows photographed in quite different circumstances above. c1892. *Kennet & Avon Canal Trust Collection*

104 A maintenance gang work their way from Winsley Bridge towards Avoncliffe, perhaps getting to their 'station' before the Whitsuntide stoppage. On the other side of the bridge there was yet another quarry wharf, Murhill. The quarry above, near Winsley, was opened in 1803 after it was realised that the Conkwell stone (see caption 97) was inferior and was linked to the canal by a wooden railroad. The same year Rennie was clearly getting exasperated with the poor quality of the local stone when he wrote to the Canal Committee thus:

> 'Seeing the great Loss that the Company have sustained and the great detention which the Works have experienced from the badness of the Stone, I feel it my duty to repeat again to the Committee, what I have frequently done before, the propriety of again considering whether it would not be better to use Bricks generally, instead of Stone in the Works which are yet to do.'

Despite Rennies's plea, stone continued to be the main construction material and things only improved after 1808 when stone from Bathampton Down was made more accessible (see caption 93). c1910. *Kennet & Avon Canal Trust Collection*

105 & 106 Avoncliff Aqueduct is longer than its western neighbour, Dundas; its imperfections – and in particular its centre sag – are thus the more obvious. Avoncliff suffered more than Dundas from the use of inferior stone, indeed it was problems with this and the two smaller aqueducts east of Bradford-on-Avon, Biss and Semington, that forced the Canal Company to seek other sources. The track that sweeps round from the aqueduct in the above photograph took waggons carrying stone down to a railway siding. The stone came from Randell, Saunders & Co's quarry on the hill above at Westwood and was also loaded onto boats at a wharf on the far side of the aqueduct.

Avoncliff's canalside community has its origins in the local cloth trade as evidenced by the two flock mills on the river to the left – the chimney of one is clearly visible. But the canal brought with it its own community and soon the local Cross Guns – the building just left of centre – echoed to both the old and new order. The mill nearest the canal soon took advantage of it and changed from water to steam power, its coal being delivered right to its doorstep by boat, probably by one of the local Bradford-on-Avon carriers who traded in coal from Somerset's collieries.

The second view of the aqueduct scarcely does it justice as it succumbs to the GWR's annual maintenance programme. It would seem that the rails along the towpath have just been lifted; similarly the track down from the Westwood quarry is disused and the wharfside crane gone, while below the lengthman's cottage a boat has been dragged up from the water. On the extreme right a high-powered conference seems in progress . . . its participants, GWR employees, perhaps speculating on how much longer they are going to have to suffer the indignity of being custodians of a canal! c1900 and c1910. *Kennet & Avon Canal Trust Collection* and *British Rail*

107 During the Great War the Red Cross were the unlikely owners of the narrow boat, *Bittern* – pictured here turning at Avoncliff Wharf. Wise to the recuperative powers of the canal and its environs, the Red Cross used *Bittern* to take wounded soldiers from the Old Court Hospital at Avoncliff on afternoon trips to Bradford-on-Avon and back. 1917. *Kennet & Avon Canal Trust Collection*

108 About to set off for Bath, Midland Railway's *No 2* is caught by the camera alongside Bradford-on-Avon's Lower Wharf. Clearly for the Midland there was money in carrying a human cargo – possibly an all-in-one ticket that incorporated their railway connection at Bath. There is no horse towing path between Bradford's Lower Wharf and the Frome Road Wharf above the lock, though there was a path over to the right for the crew's use only. The horse would have crossed the road above while the boat was working through the lock. Digging of the western end of canal began at Bradford in 1794 and the wharf here was a natural development of this; when the lock was completed the Frome Road Wharf became the more important as there was a gauging dock (for calculating tolls) alongside the warehouse – the roof of which can just be seen at the top right.

In terms of usage, it appears that the more established carriers such as Betts & Drewe, Shaw & Co, C & R Parker (whose agent here was Henry Sainsbury, later of Gerrish & Sainsbury), Gerrish & Co and the Midland Railway were based above the lock, while more locally-based carriers and coal merchants were based at the Lower Wharf. As at Bath, the Bradford wharves soon became also the domain of local families that maintained, often through successive generations, close contact with the canal and its trade. Ebenezer Chapman was the Canal Company's agent and toll collector for some 40 years while the Edmunds family were involved in boat-building and ran Lower Wharf's adjacent hostelry, the Canal Tavern. Similarly, in the latter part of the 19th century, the landlord of the Barge (above the lock), W Norris, dabbled in carrying on the canal. In 1875 local smith and farrier, H A Summers, began carrying coal from the Somerset collieries to Lower Wharf for the nearby Gas & Coke Company in the narrow boats *Jack Tar, Tiger* and *Leopard*; the trade ceased with the closure of the SCC in 1898. Likewise, coal merchant James Randall tried unsuccessfully to seek alternative trade for his boats, *Sarah Ann* and *Eliza* when the link with Somerset's coal was severed. In 1902 *Eliza* was taken on by Thomas Powell of Seend to join *Sir Daniel* bought the previous year; in 1904 Powell took over the Bradford-on-Avon end of Henry Gerrish's business and subsequently added the fly-boat *Knott* to his small fleet but had ceased carrying by the end of the Great War.
c1910. *Kennet & Avon Canal Trust Collection*

109 The party from Trowbridge, first encountered in photograph 97, pole their way out of Bradford Lock towards Lower Wharf where their horse awaits. The unnamed boat probably belongs to Thomas Powell (see caption 108) who, alone at the time, was still operating locally. c1910. *Kennet & Avon Canal Trust Collection*

Map 1: *Bristol to Kelston Lock*
Photographs 1 – 54

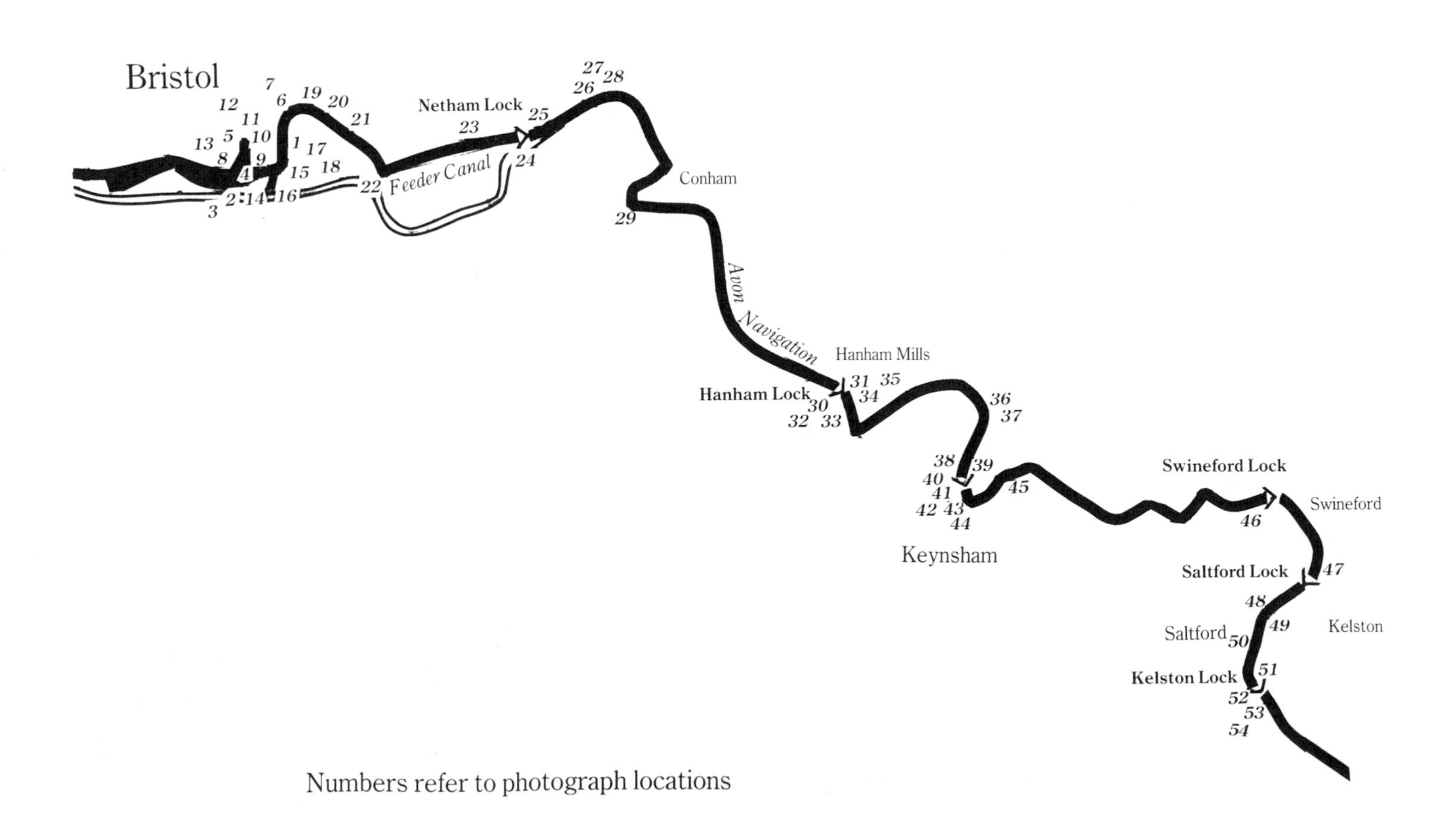

Numbers refer to photograph locations

Map 2: *Kelston to Bradford-on-Avon*
Photographs 55 – 109

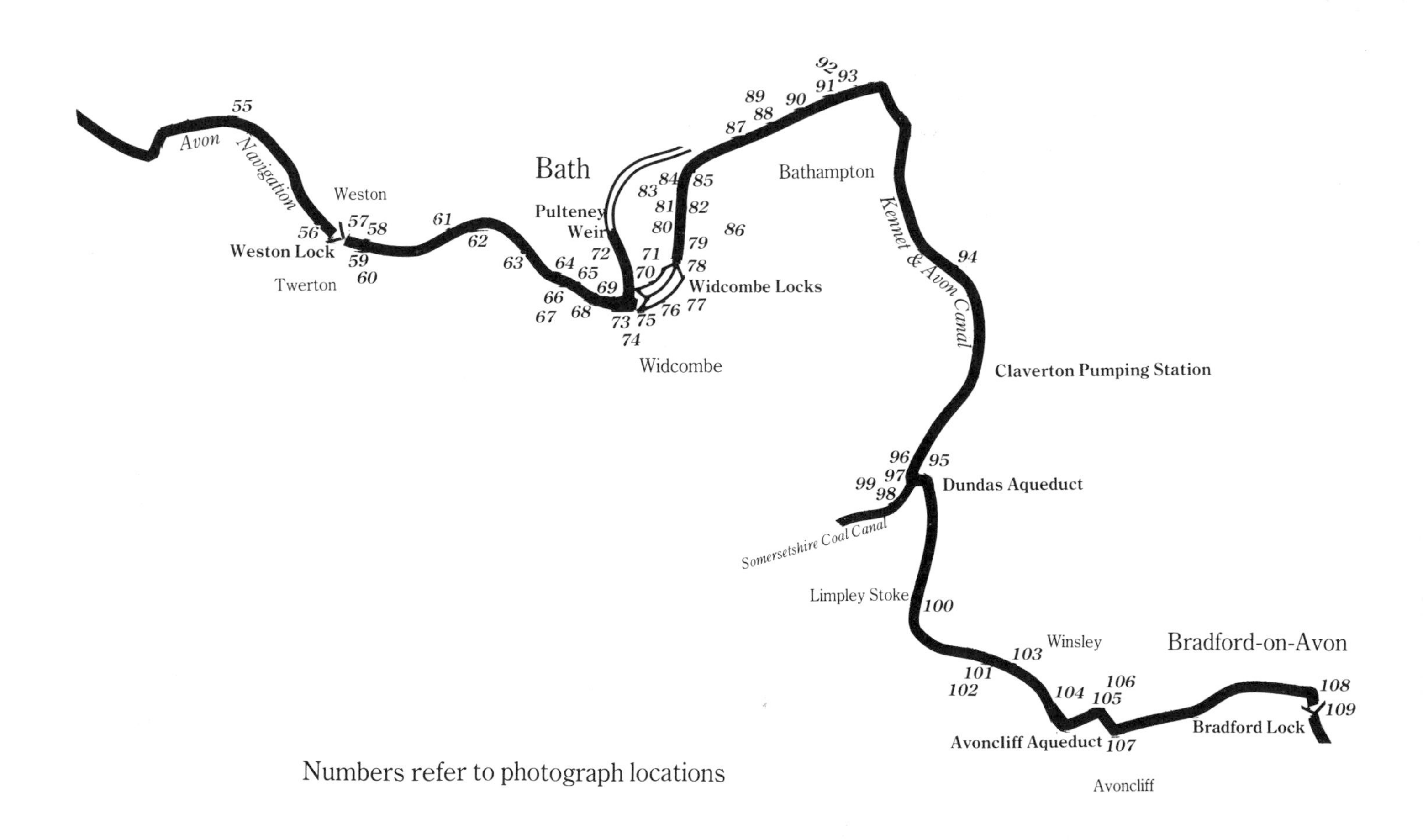

Numbers refer to photograph locations

ACKNOWLEDGEMENTS

. . . **for their first-hand experiences** I am indebted to Jim Crissup, Albert and Phyllis Head, George Head, Bob Blackwell, Hubert Ashmead and James Cole.

. . . **for their research facilities and patience** I am most grateful to the staff of Bath Reference Library, Bath Lending Library, Victoria Art Gallery, Bath City Archives, Bath Industrial Heritage Centre, Bristol Reference Library, Bristol Record Office, Port of Bristol Authority, Wiltshire Library & Museum Service, Devizes Reference Library and British Rail Record Office.

. . . **for their previously published researches,** the following authors have been invaluable sources:
Kenneth R Clew: *The Kennet & Avon Canal,* David & Charles.
Joan Day: *Bristol Brass: a History of the Industry,* David & Charles.
Grahame Farr: *Ship-building in the Port of Bristol,* National Maritime Museum.
Harold Fassnidge & Peter Maundrell: *Bradford-on-Avon, a pictorial record,* Wiltshire Library & Museum Service.
John Latimer: *Annals of Bristol.*
John Lord & Jem Southam: The Floating Harbour: A landscape history of Bristol City Docks, Redcliffe Press.
Maurice Scott: *Discovering Widcombe and Lyncombe, Bath,* Maurice Scott.
Percy Sims: *A History of Saltford Village,* P T Sims & R M Mawditt.
Hugh Torrens: *The Evolution of a Family Firm: Stothert & Pitt,* Stothert & Pitt.

. . . **for their expertise in specific areas** thanks to John Barriscale (Stothert & Pitt), Tony Brown (Keynsham and Saltford), Harold Fassnidge (Bradford-on-Avon), P J C Harbutt (Harbutt's Plasticine), Brian Milsom (South-West Gas and William Butler & Co), Maurice Scott (Widcombe).

. . . **for permission to use their photographs and/or prints,** special thanks to Hubert Ashmead, Bob Blackwell, Tony Brown, James Cole, John Cornwell, Chris Gibson, Albert Head, Brian Milsom, Maurice Scott, Tim Wheeldon, Bath City Council, Bath Reference Library, British Rail Records Office, Kennet & Avon Canal Trust, Port of Bristol Authority, Victoria Art Gallery and Wiltshire Library & Museum Service.

. . . **for their practical advice and assistance** Sarah Barnes, Julie Brewer, Steve Chandler and John Sansom were invaluable allies.

. . . **and for being there with their friendship** I shall always be indebted to Kay Bowen, Jan Keen, Margo Jackson, Tony Jackson, Sandra Marsh, Sylvie Meadows and Lloyd de la Mille.

REDCLIFFE BOOKS
A Selection

IMAGES OF BRISTOL
Victorian photographers at work 1850–1910
James Belsey and David Harrison

This selection of outstanding Victorian and Edwardian photographs provides a living portrait of an historic city in the nineteenth century, and shows the Victorians' fascination with the romantic image, street life, invention and industry.

Essays trace the development of the camera, and show how the pioneers first emulated and developed the style and subject matter of the artist, and then found the material – such as the tightly packed streets of the inner city – which best suited the new medium.

247mm × 232mm **104pp** **Paperbound**
ISBN 0 948265 26 4 **£5.95**

BRUNEL'S KINGDOM
Photography and the making of history
Rob Powell

Using Brunel and his works as a starting-point, this is an examination of how early photography represented the Victorian world, particularly the world of industry and engineering which was Brunel's sphere of activity and influence.

The book then traces how that representation influenced our own, subsequent views of the period.

Published with Watershed Media Centre.

208mm × 270mm **80pp** **Paperbound**
ISBN 0 951053 90 6 **£4.95**

BRUNEL'S BRISTOL
Angus Buchanan and Michael Williams

The first full study of the impact on Bristol of the celebrated Victorian engineer, with special reference to Clifton Suspension Bridge, s.s. Great Britain and Temple Meads Railway Station.

It tells of Brunel's triumphs, exasperations and disappointments in the city which, as a young man, he adopted as his own and which he continued to regard with affection for the rest of his life.

235mm × 175mm 96pp 60 illustrations **Casebound and paperbound editions**
ISBN 0 905459 39 3 £6.95 **ISBN 0 905459 45 8 £4.50**

THE FLOATING HARBOUR

A landscape history of Bristol City Docks

John Lord and Jem Southam

The first published study of Bristol's historic City Docks. John Lord describes the development of the landscape of the docks since the construction, early in the last century, of the deep-water Floating Harbour. The port's architecture and scenery are subjected to lively comment.

Jem Southam's superb photographs provide a unique and definitive contemporary portrait of the harbour, and capture the rich and varied texture of its surviving fabric. The book also includes a number of rare views of the port in the 1920s and 1930s, several maps and a gazeteer.

203mm × 250mm **128pp** **83 b/w photographs**
ISBN 0 905459 68 7 **£7.50**

All available from booksellers, but in case of difficulty please write to the publishers, Redcliffe Press Ltd, 49 Park Street, Bristol BS1 5NT, cash with order, including £1 carriage for a single copy, or 75p carriage per copy if ordering two or more.

A full catalogue of our books is available on request.

By the same author

THE KENNET & AVON CANAL: A User's Guide to the Waterways between Reading and Bristol

Niall Allsop

This fully illustrated guide to the Kennet & Avon puts the waterway in its historical and environmental context and provides a full range of advice and essential information for boater, walker and general enthusiast alike.

Millstream Books: £4.95